Butterflowers
Coloring Book

Flowers & Butterflies
Fantasy Coloring Collection

It has been such a joy putting together the designs for this coloring book. Butterflies and flowers are completely beautiful on their own, and this book brings the two together into a unique and fanciful coloring collection. These floral fantasy butterflies emerged from their cocoons bursting with flowers, swirls, hearts, leaves, and so much more. Now it's up to you to bring them to life with color. Have you ever observed the hypnotic flight of a butterfly through the garden? It's time to relax, put on some soft spa music for inspiration, and immerse yourself into the patterns, designs, and color sensations while you make your butterflowers bloom.

Your new mantra ... Butterflies and flowers and coloring for hours...

Published by Cozart Creative SM
www.cozartcreative.com

This coloring book features 40 finely detailed fanciful butterfly designs to help you indulge your colorful creative side. Each design is on one side of the page to make it easy to remove and frame your work of art. When coloring, especially when using markers or water color, we recommend placing a sheet of paper under the page to help protect the pages underneath.

Visit us at www.cozartcreative.com for information about our coloring books, articles, links to coloring tutorials, coloring supplies, and free coloring page downloads.
Browse our Etsy Shop at www.etsy.com/shop/CozartCreative to download and print individual coloring pages.

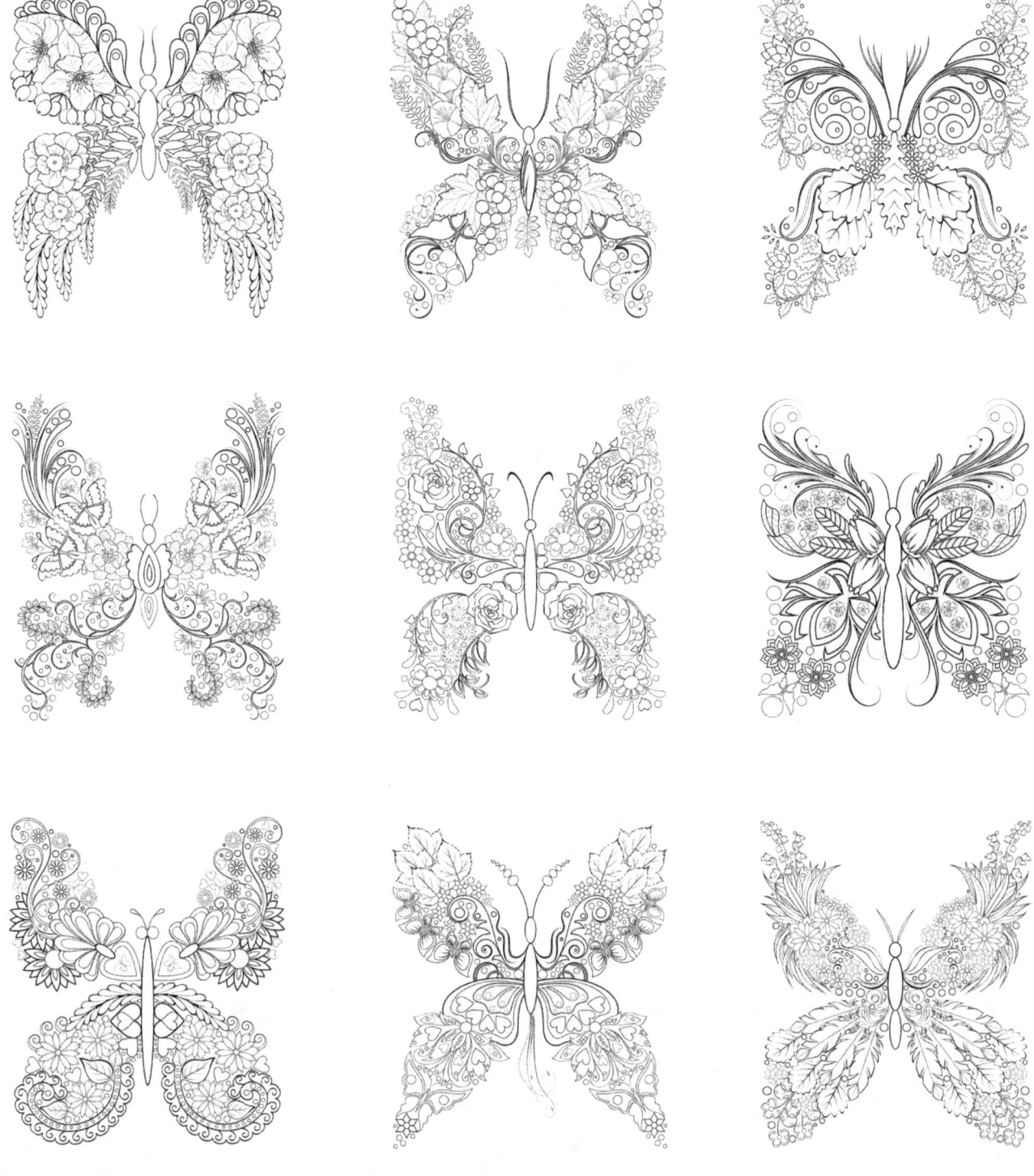

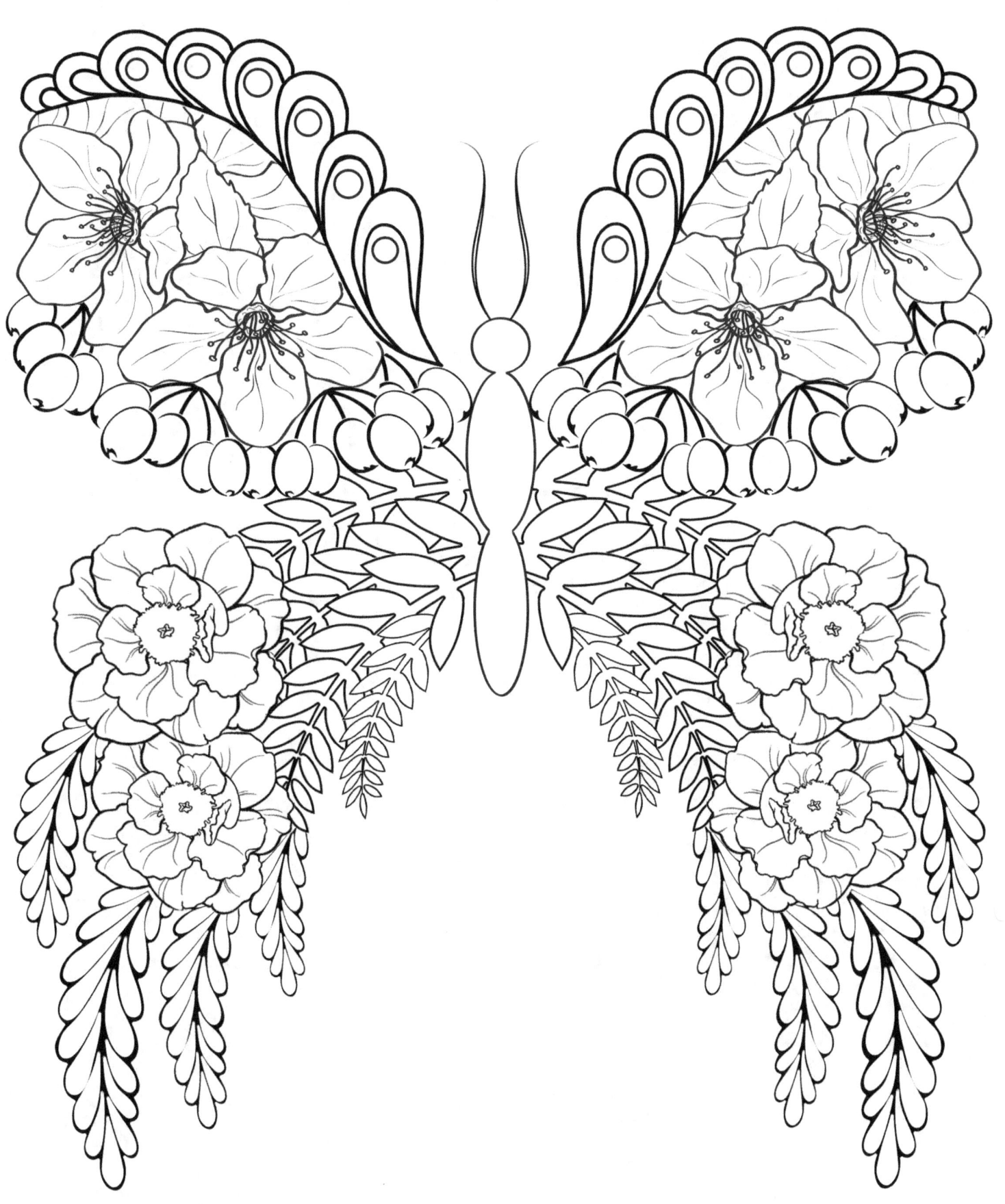

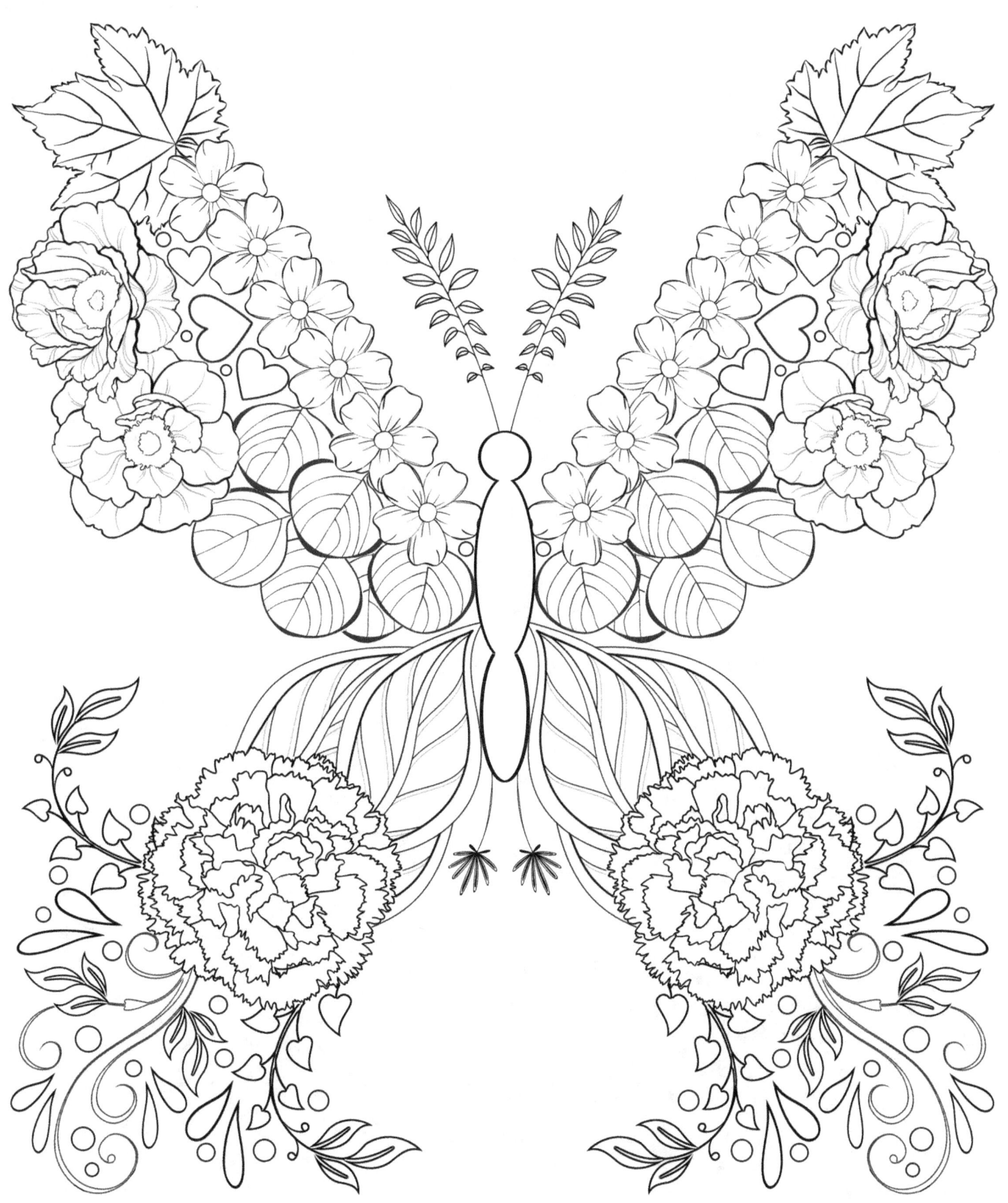

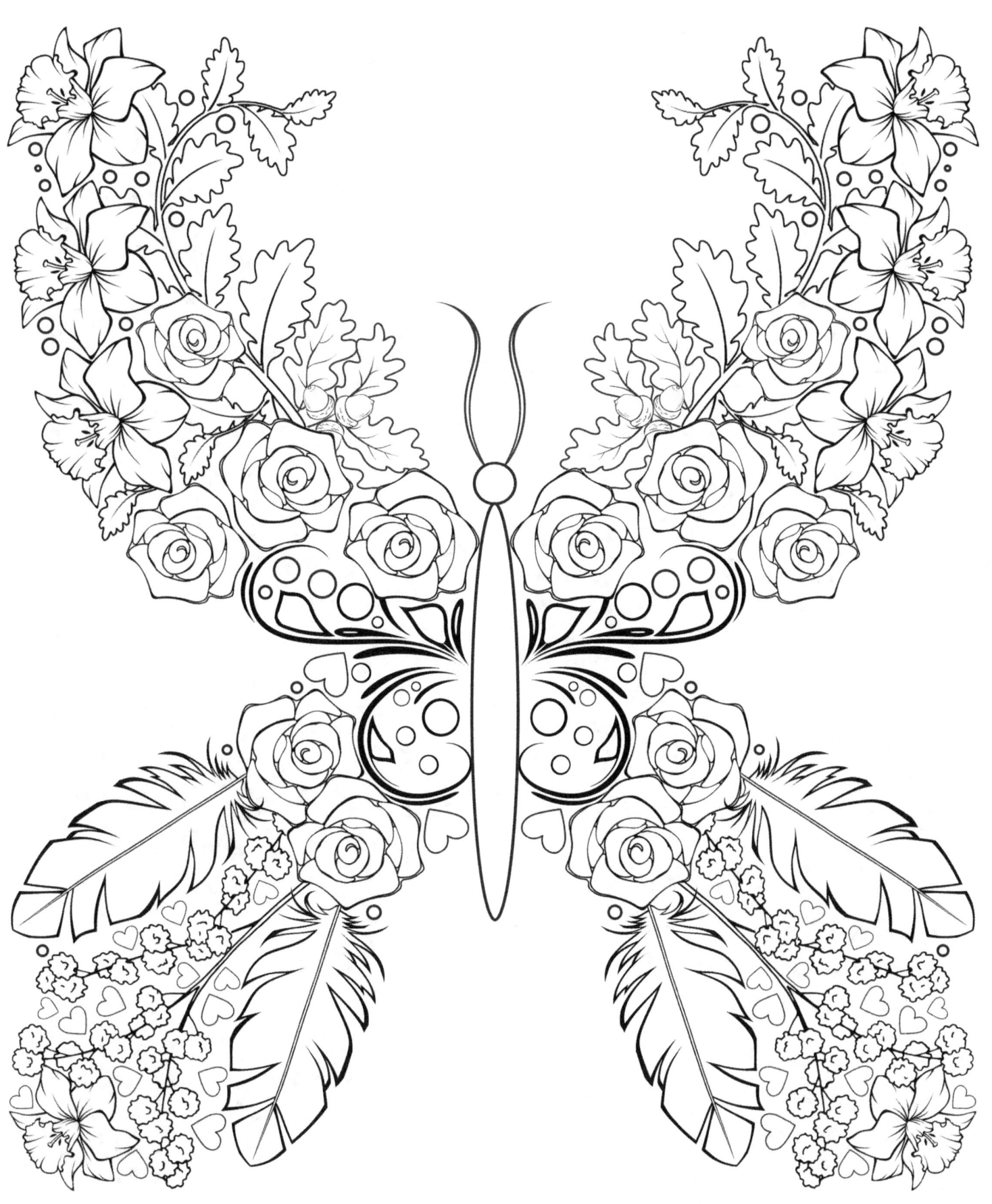

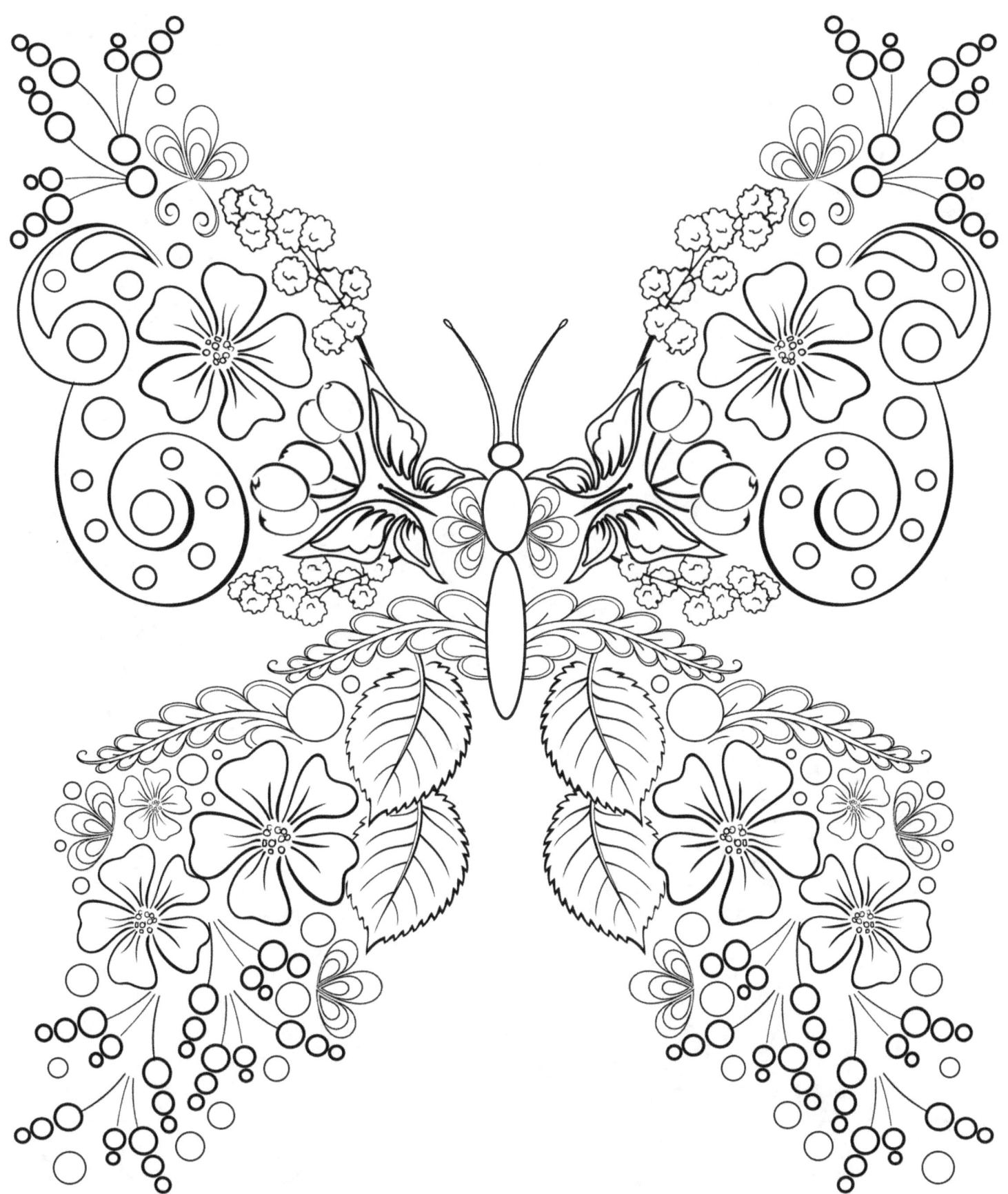

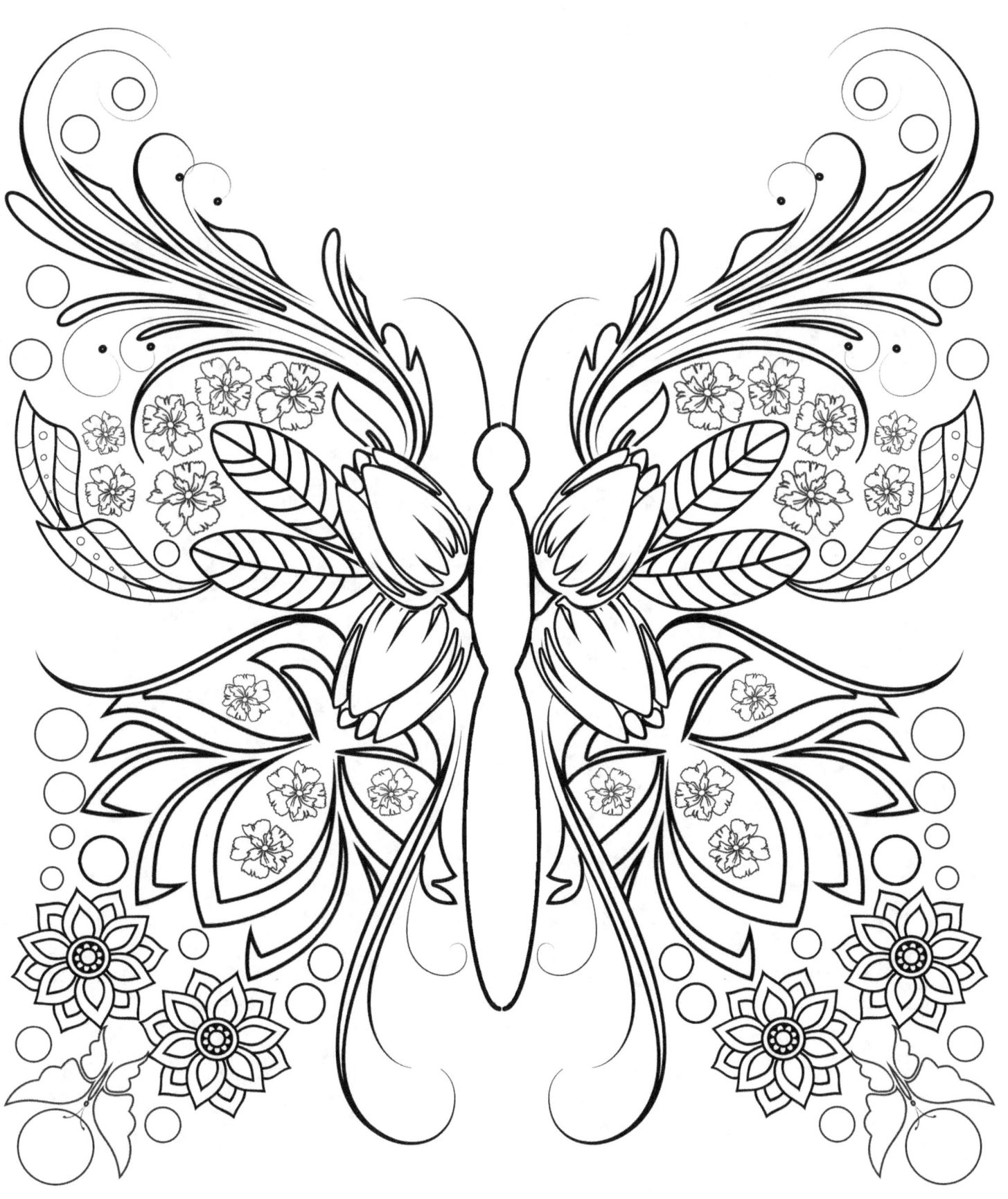

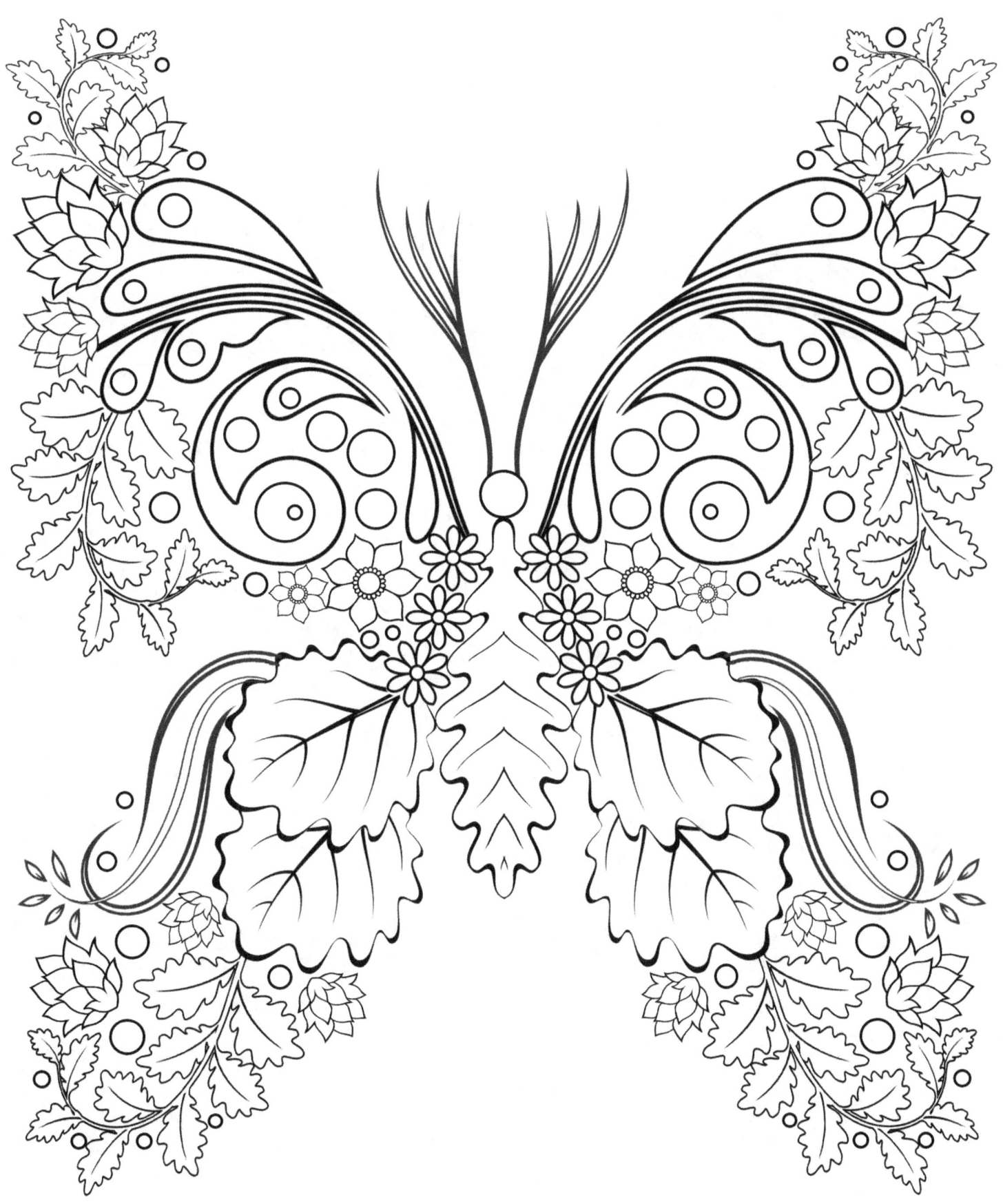

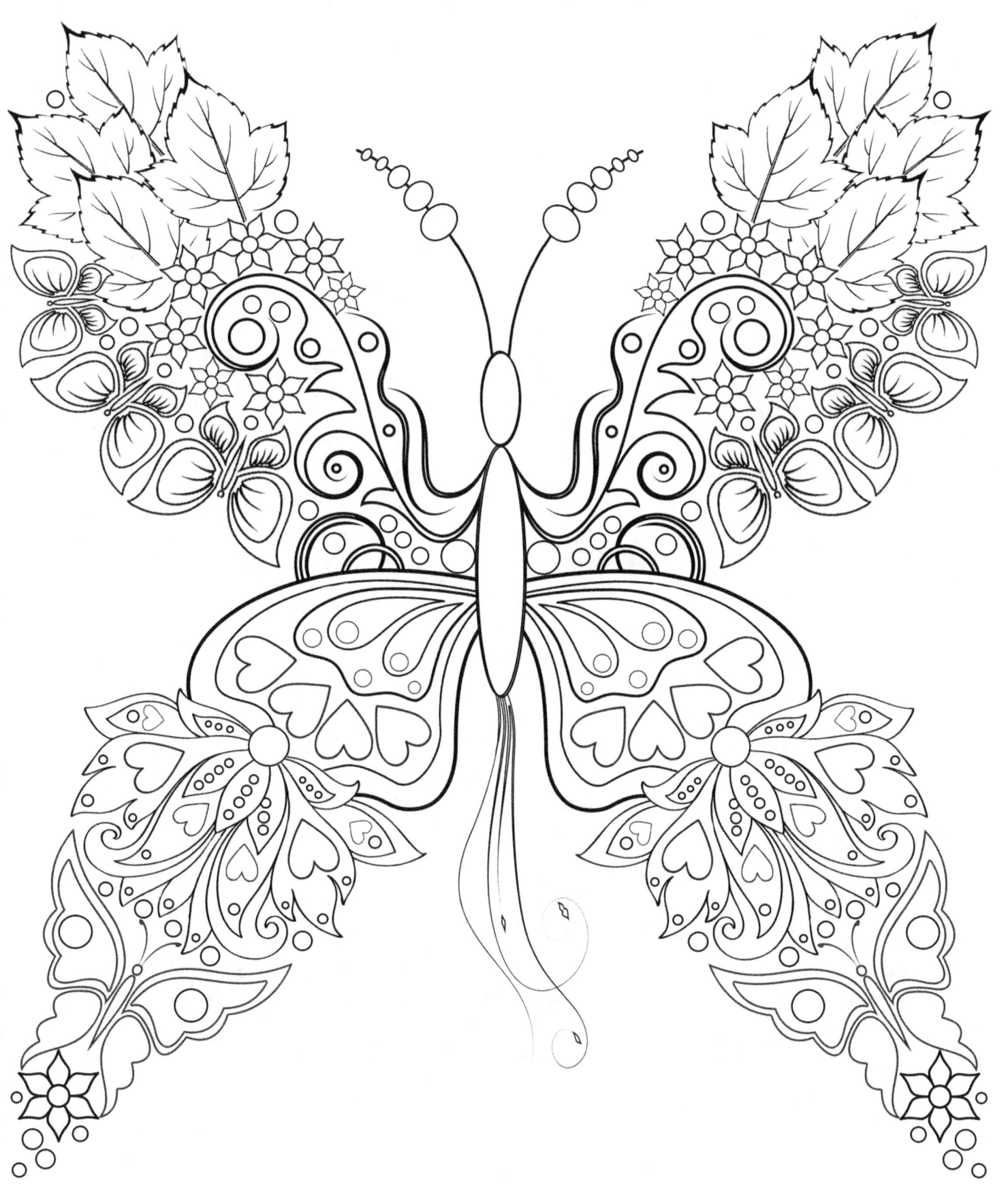

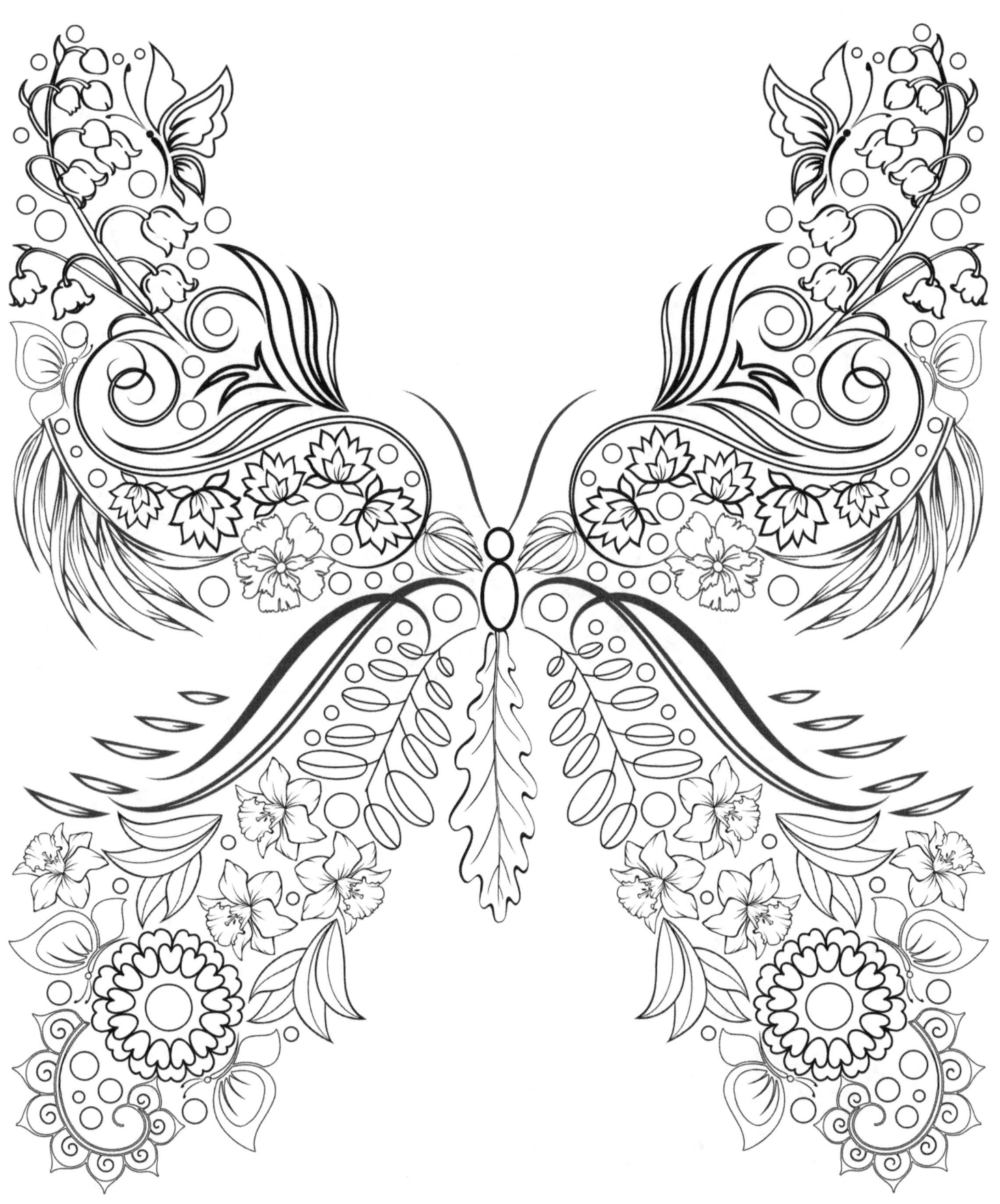

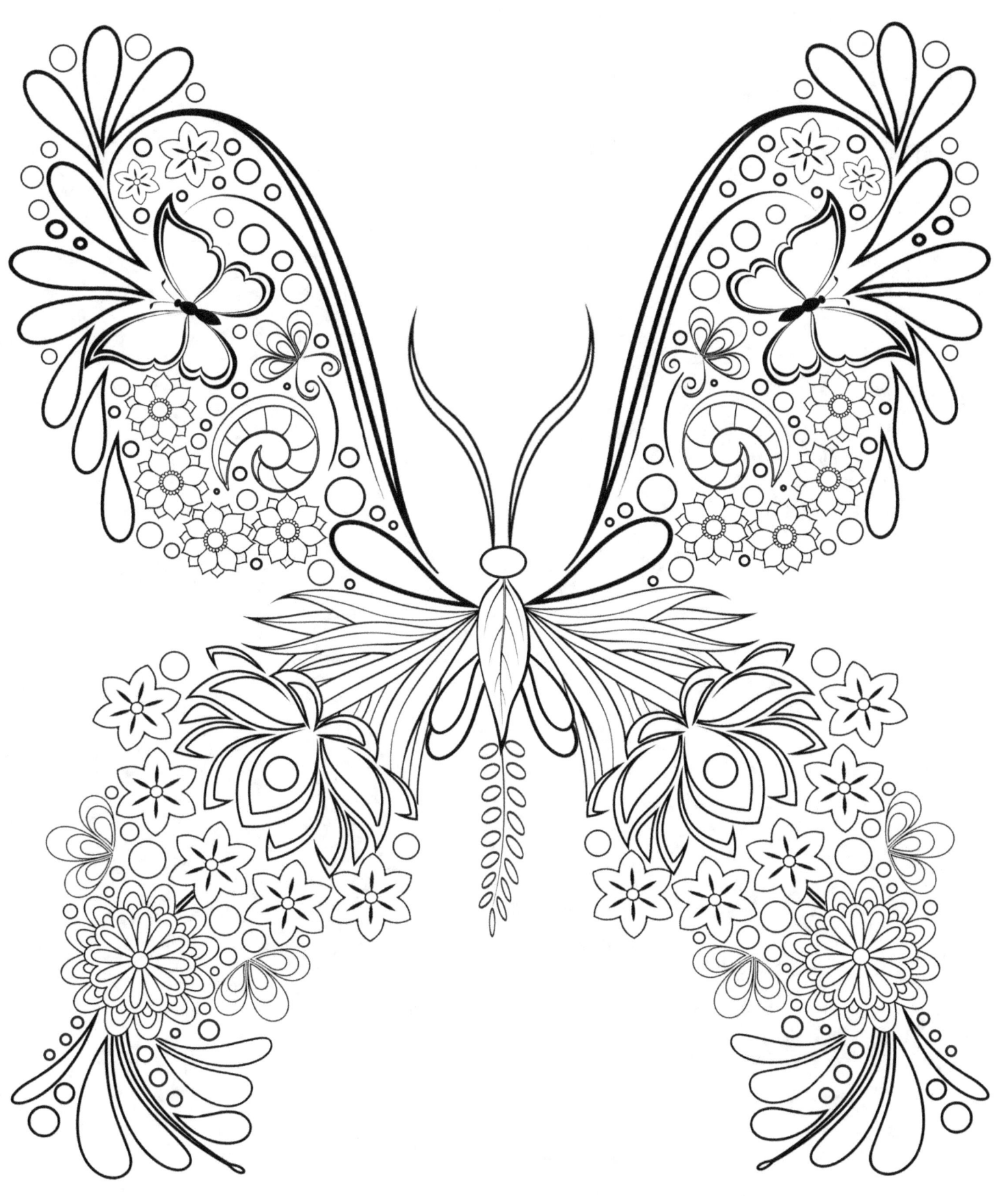

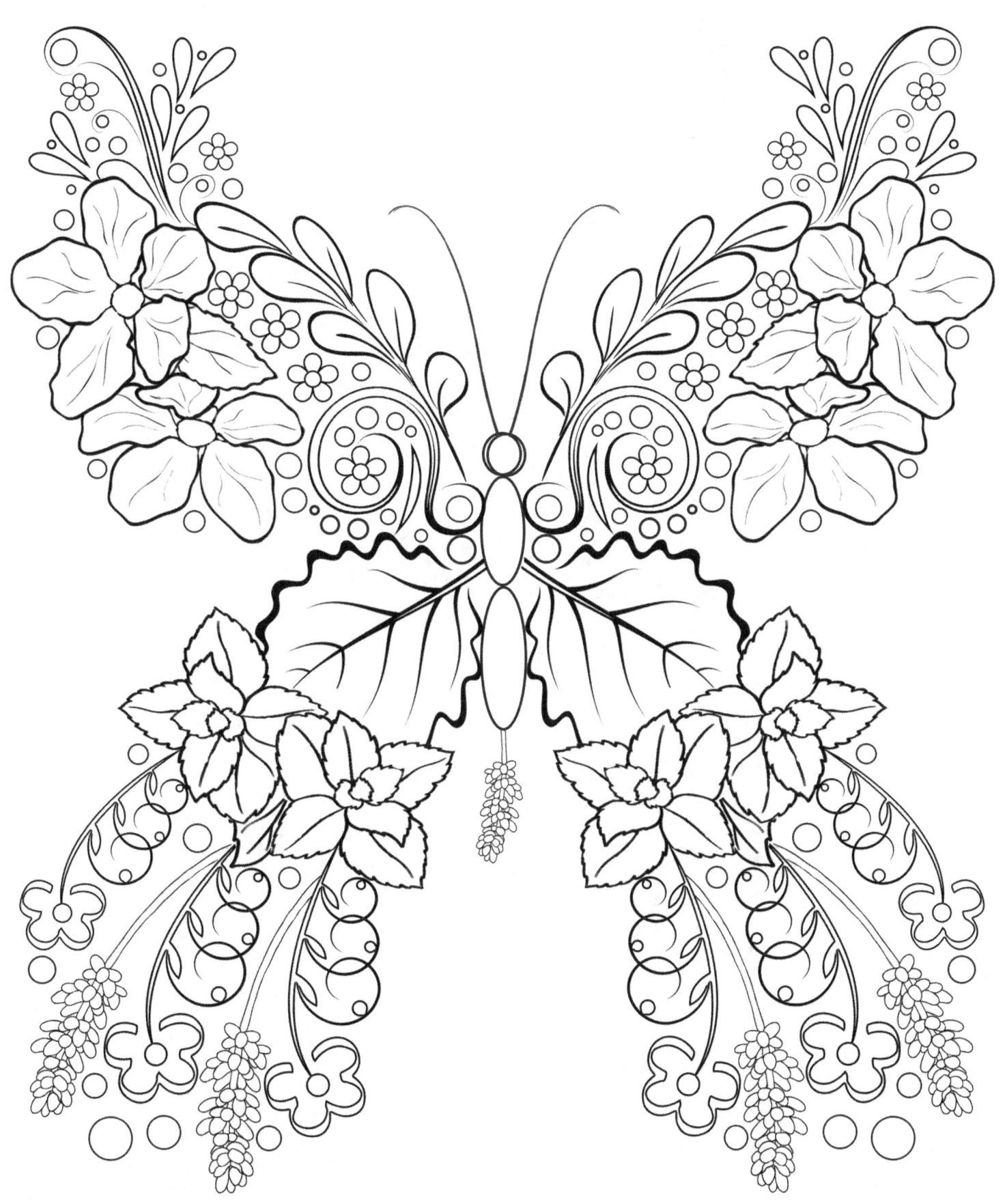

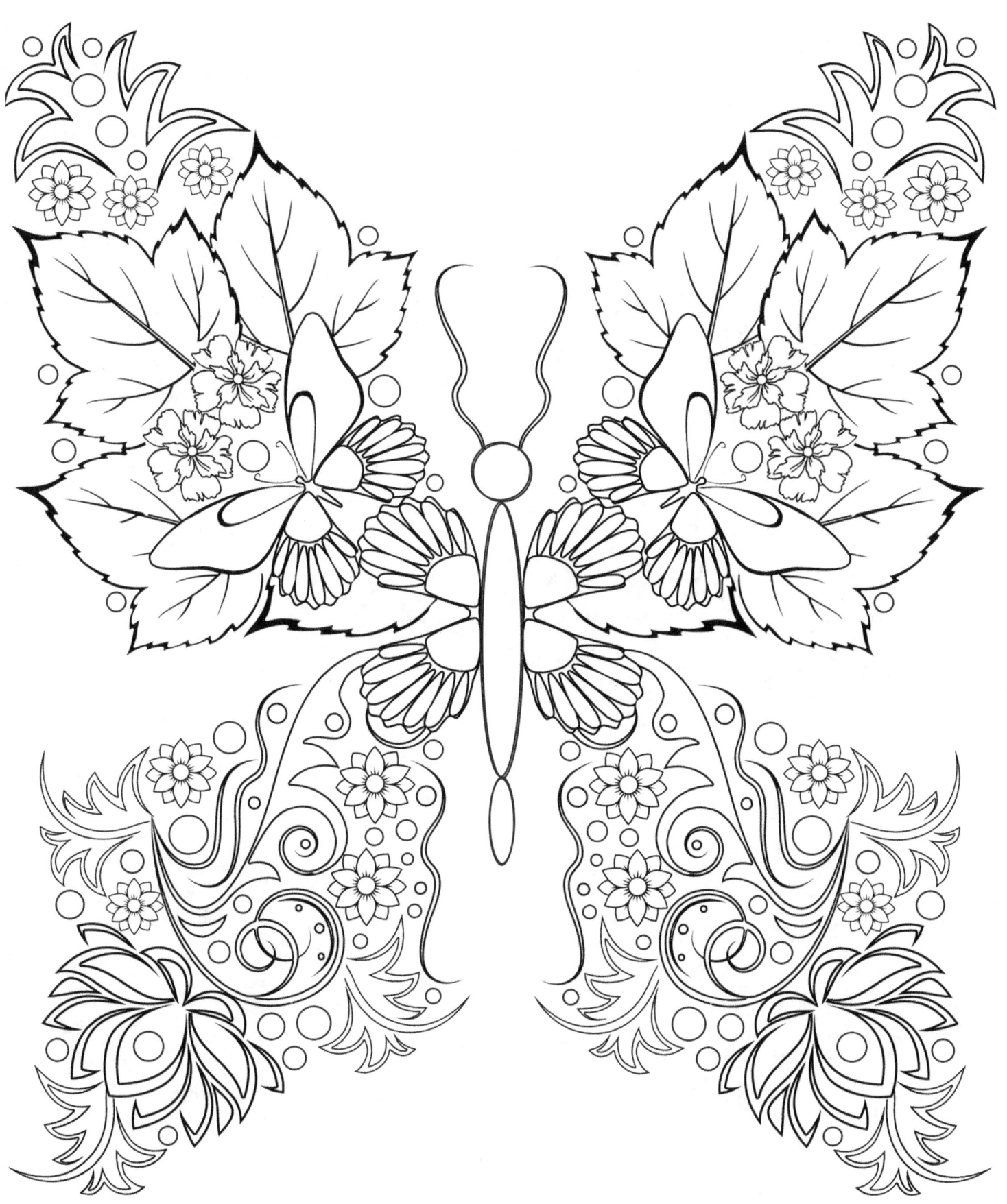

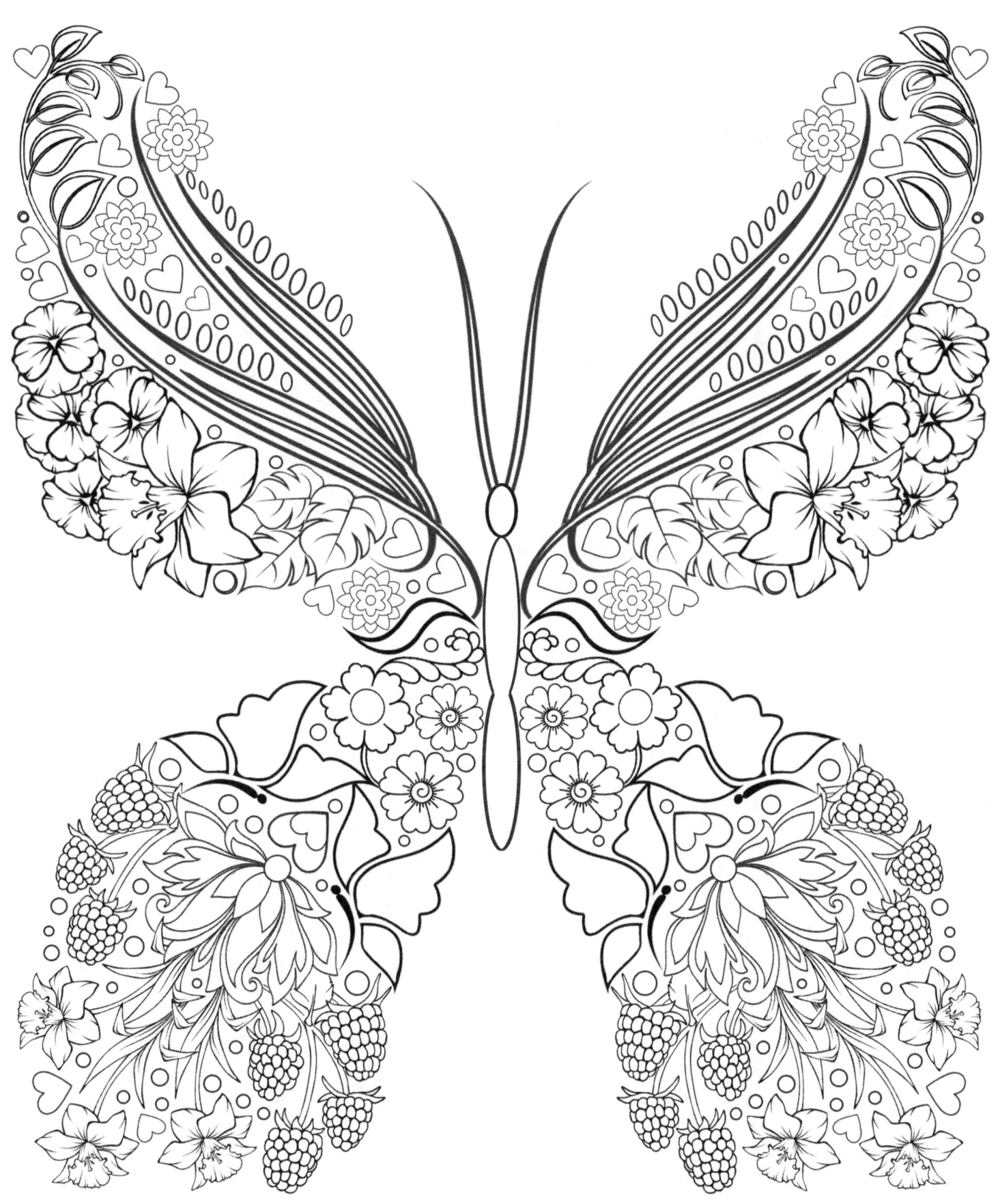

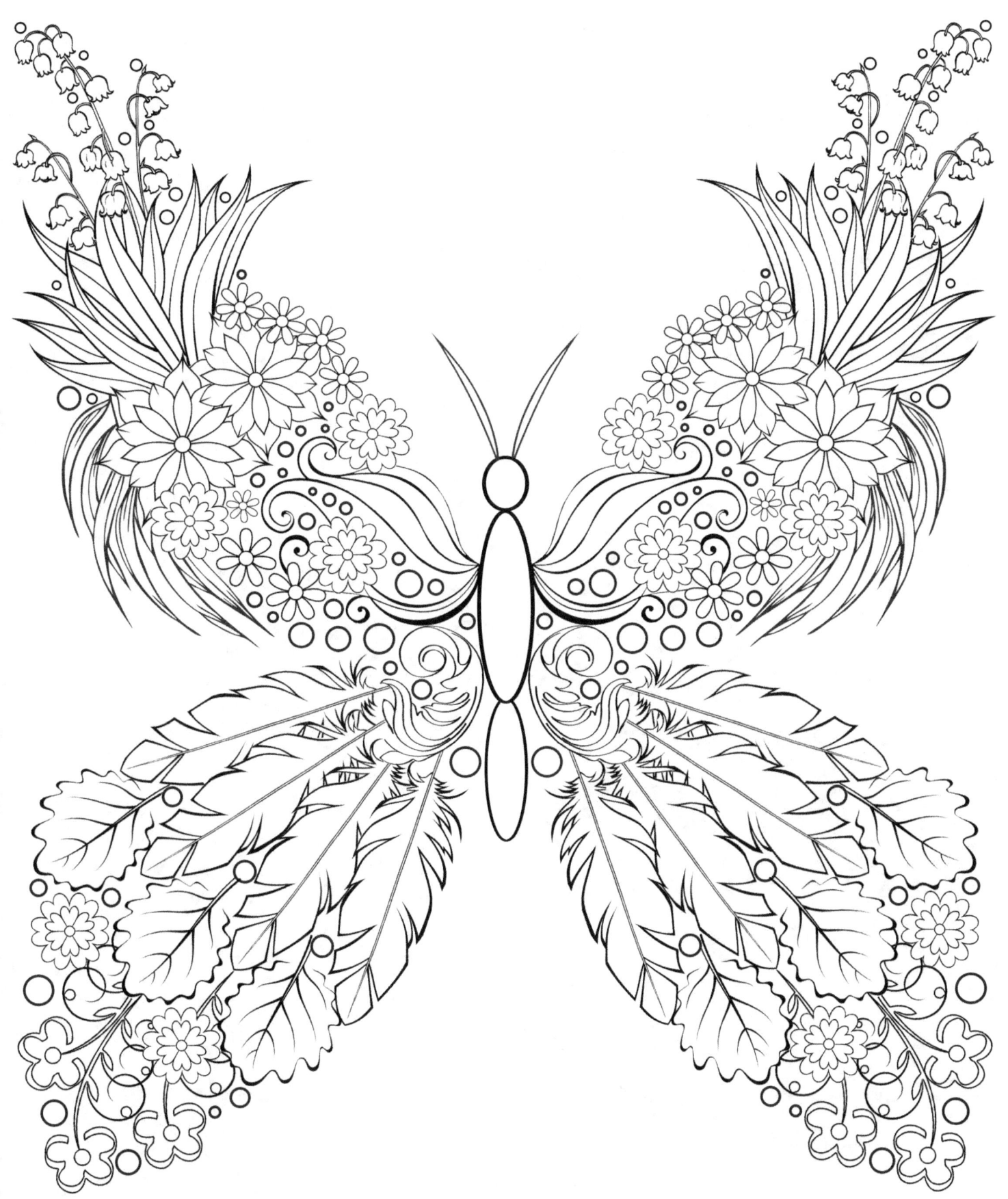

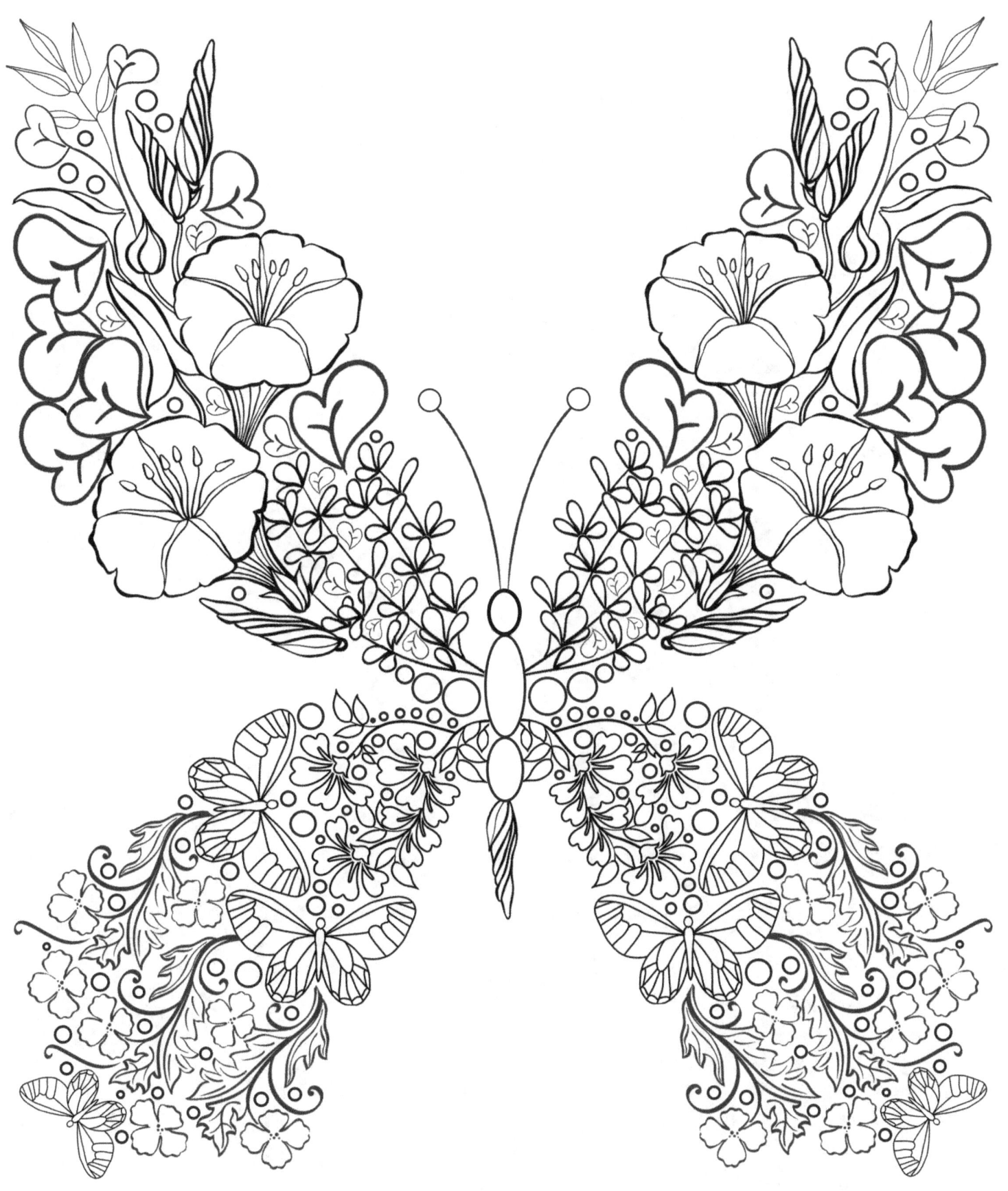

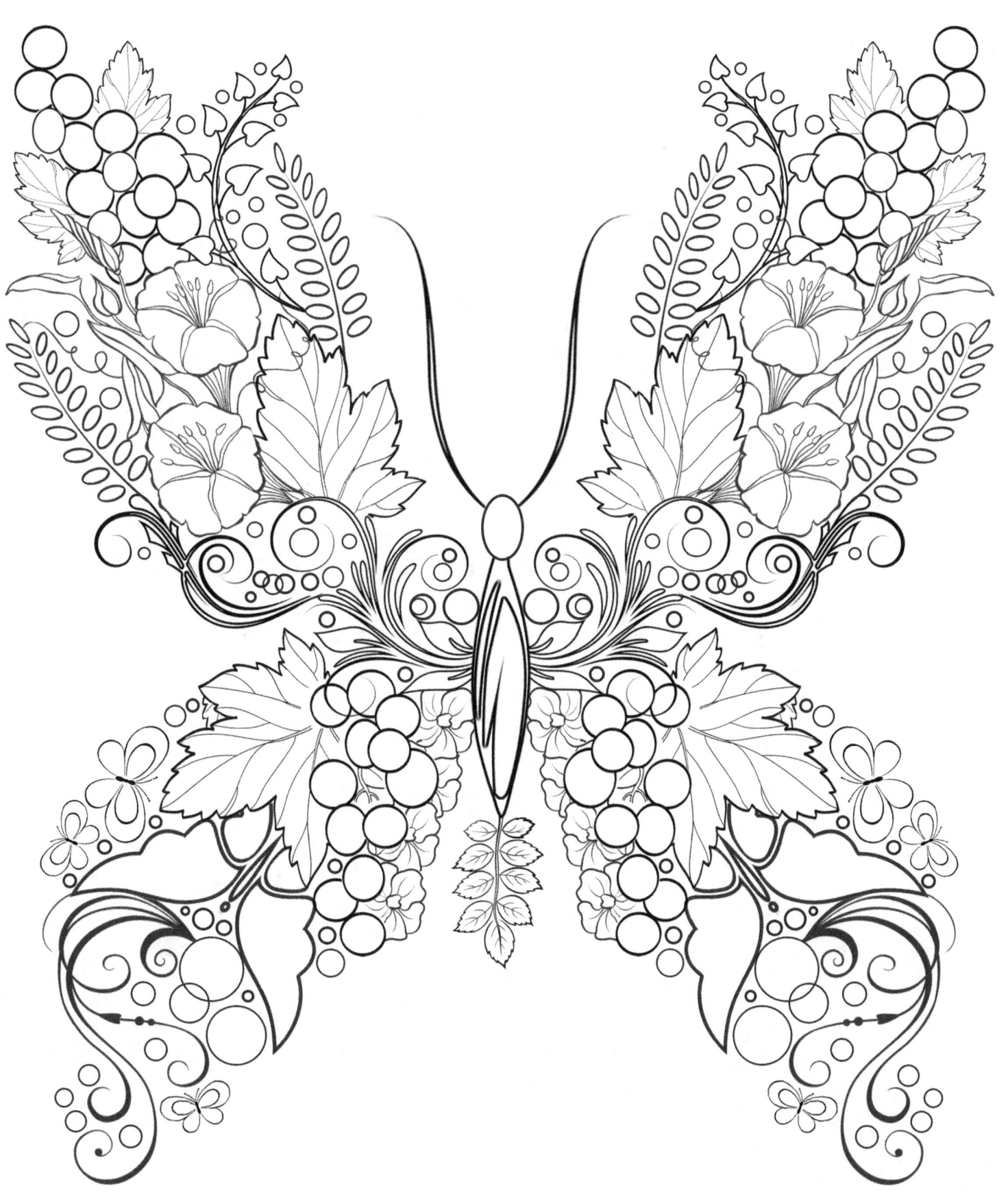

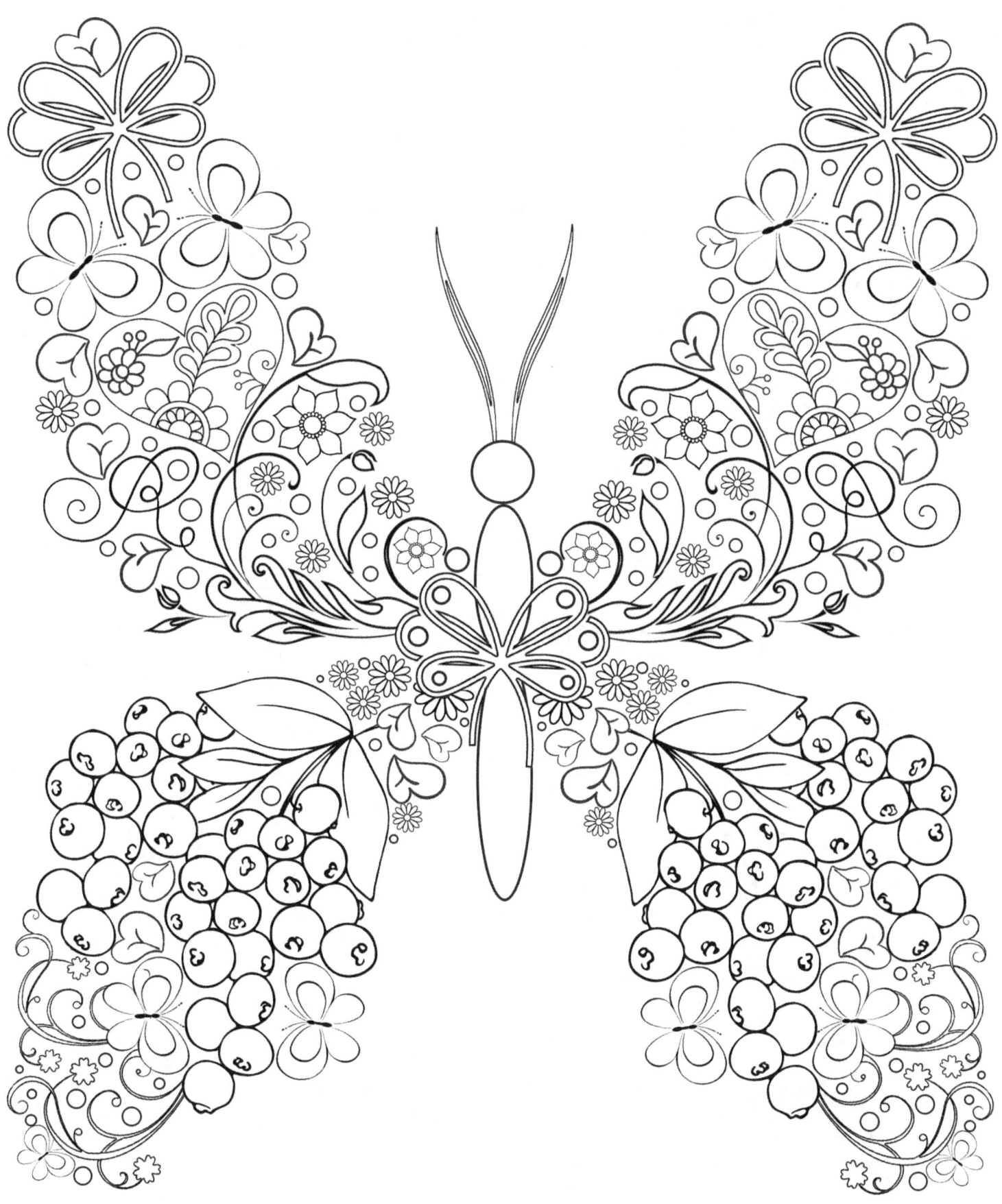

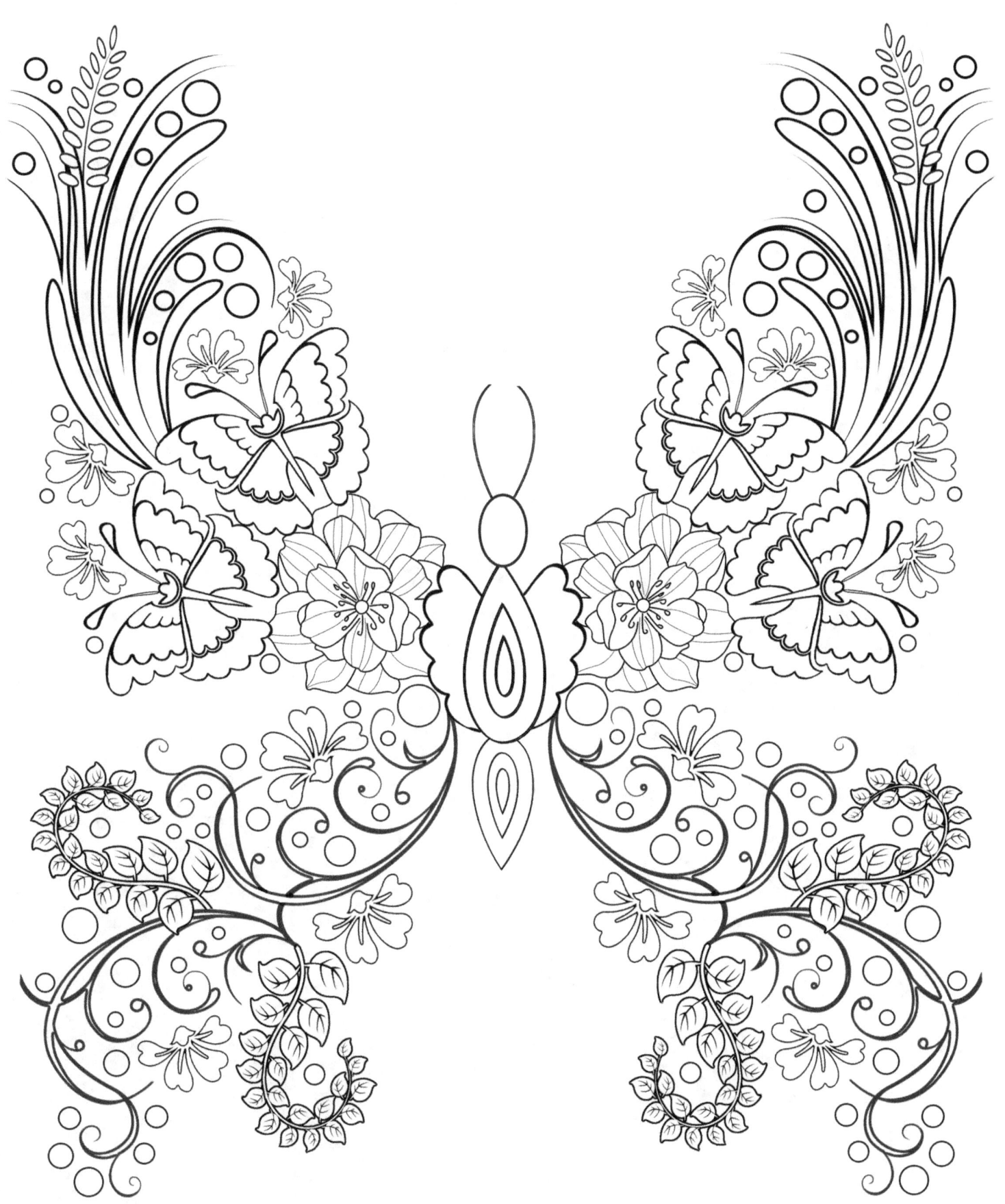

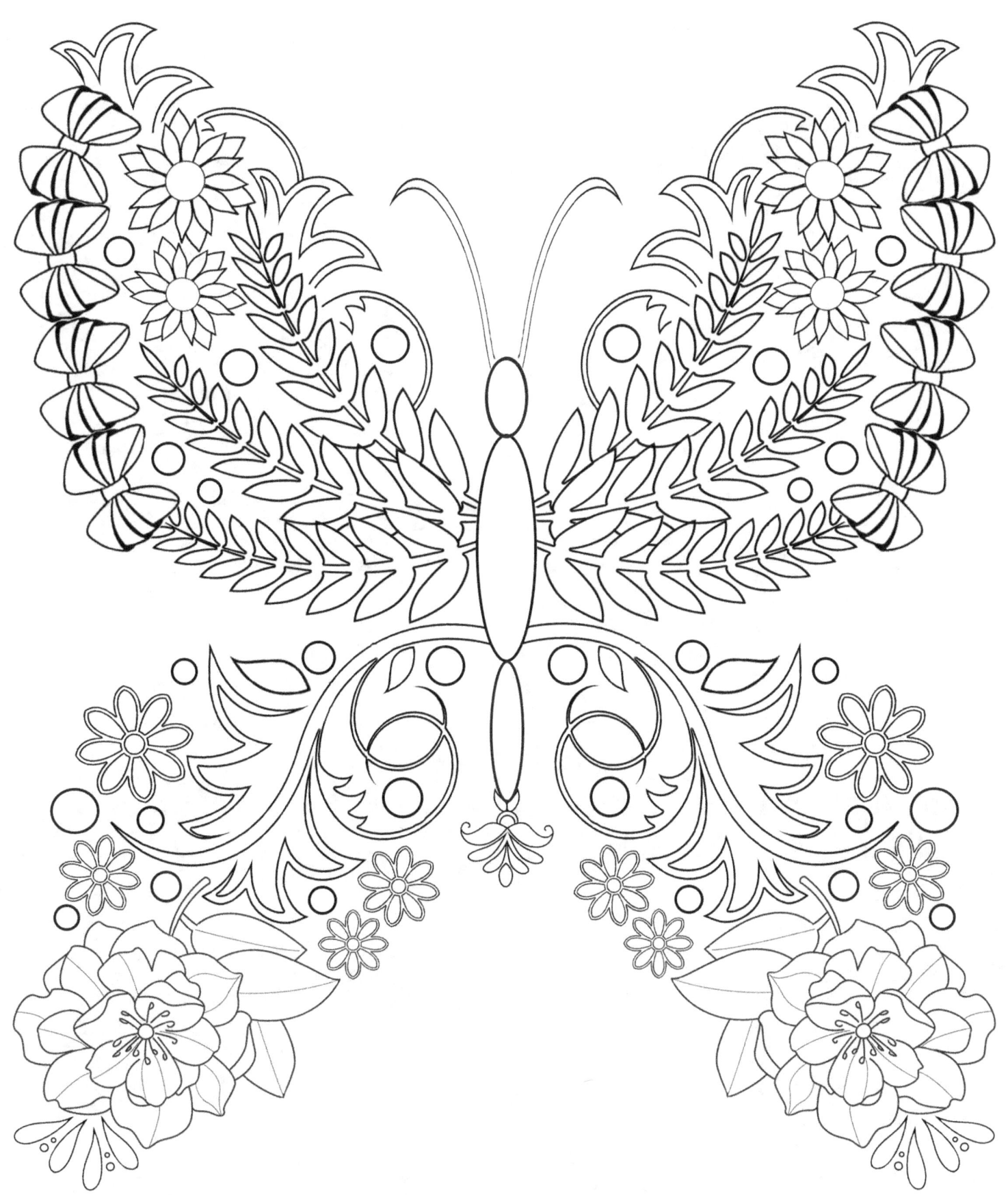

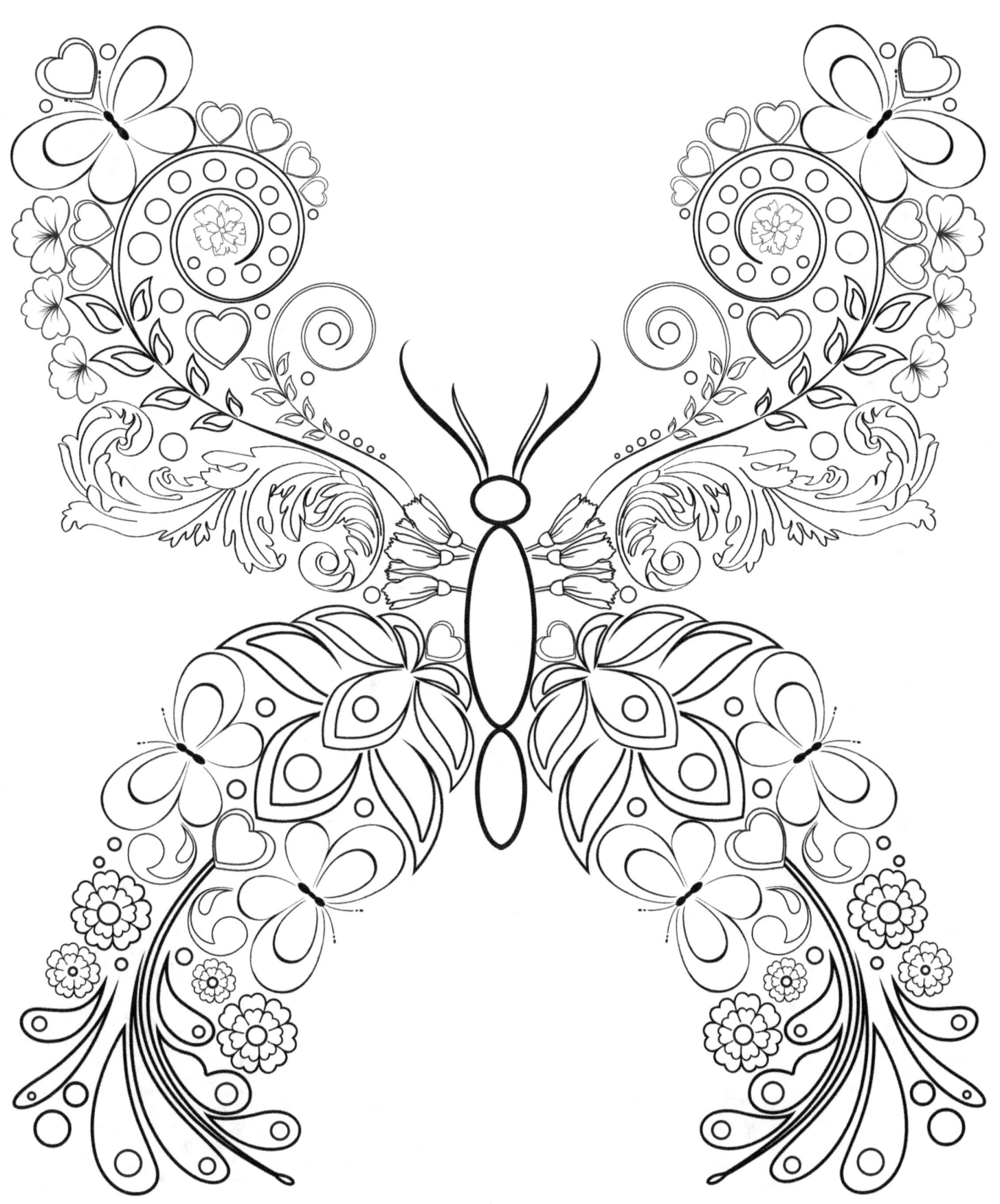

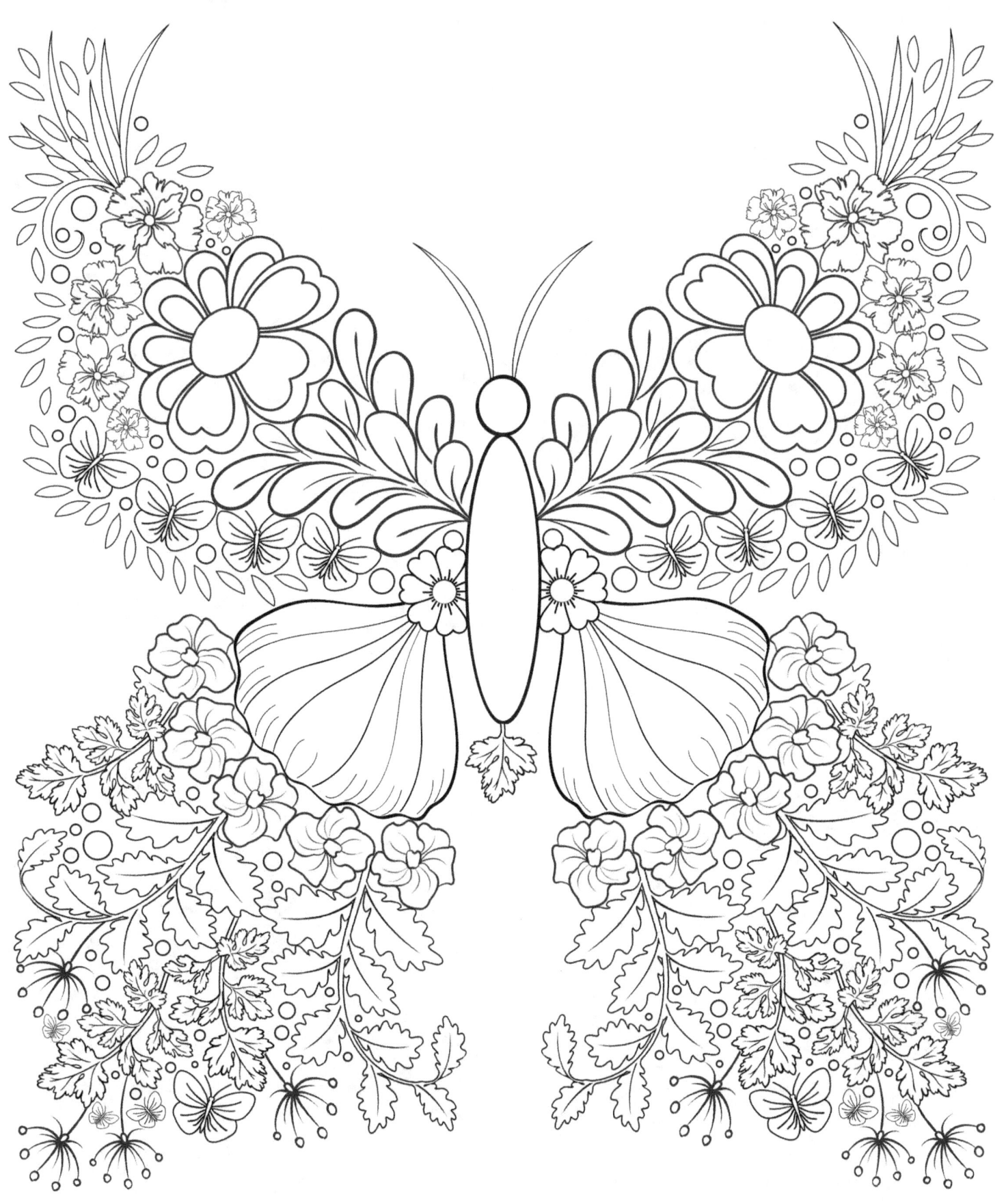

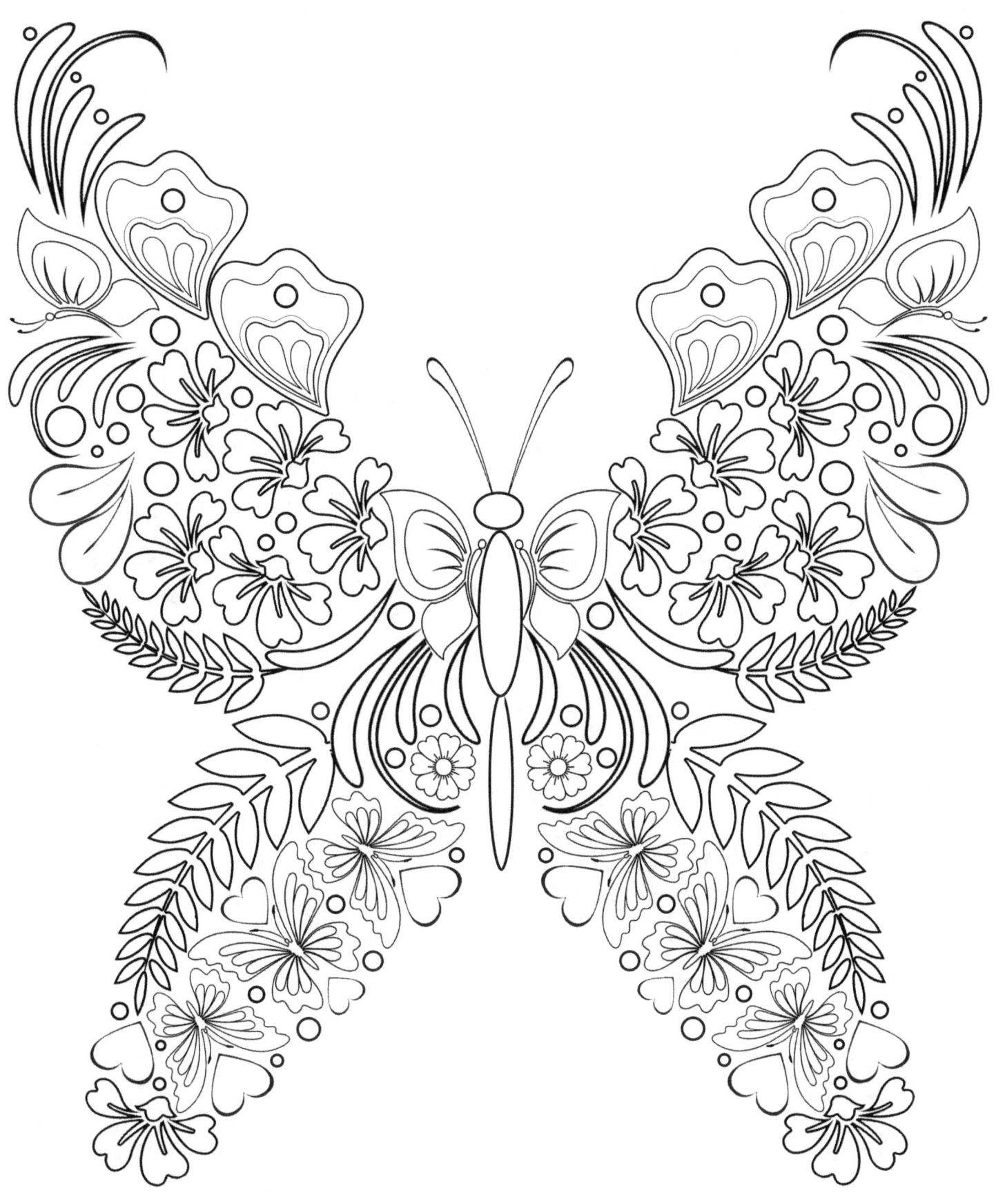

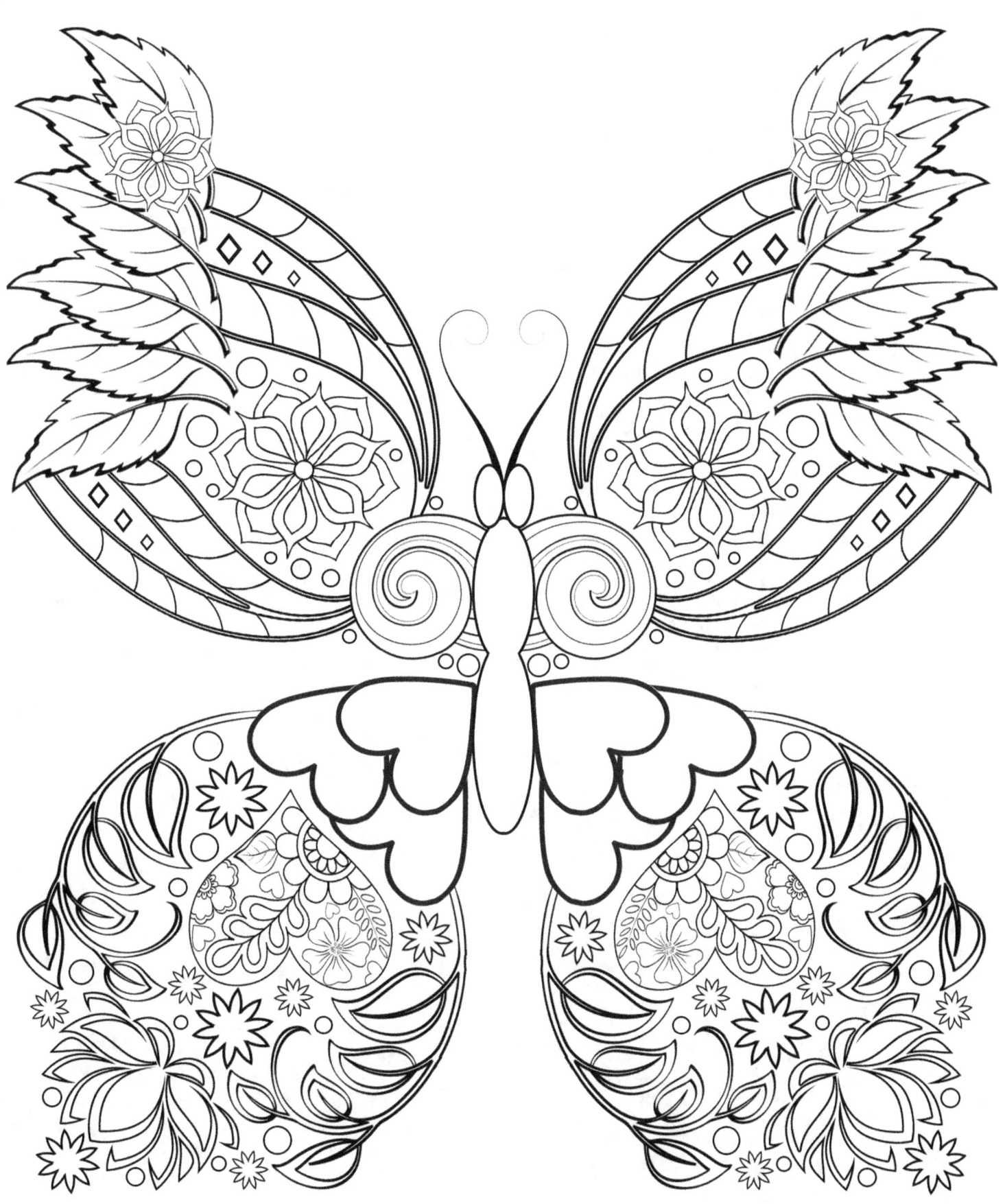

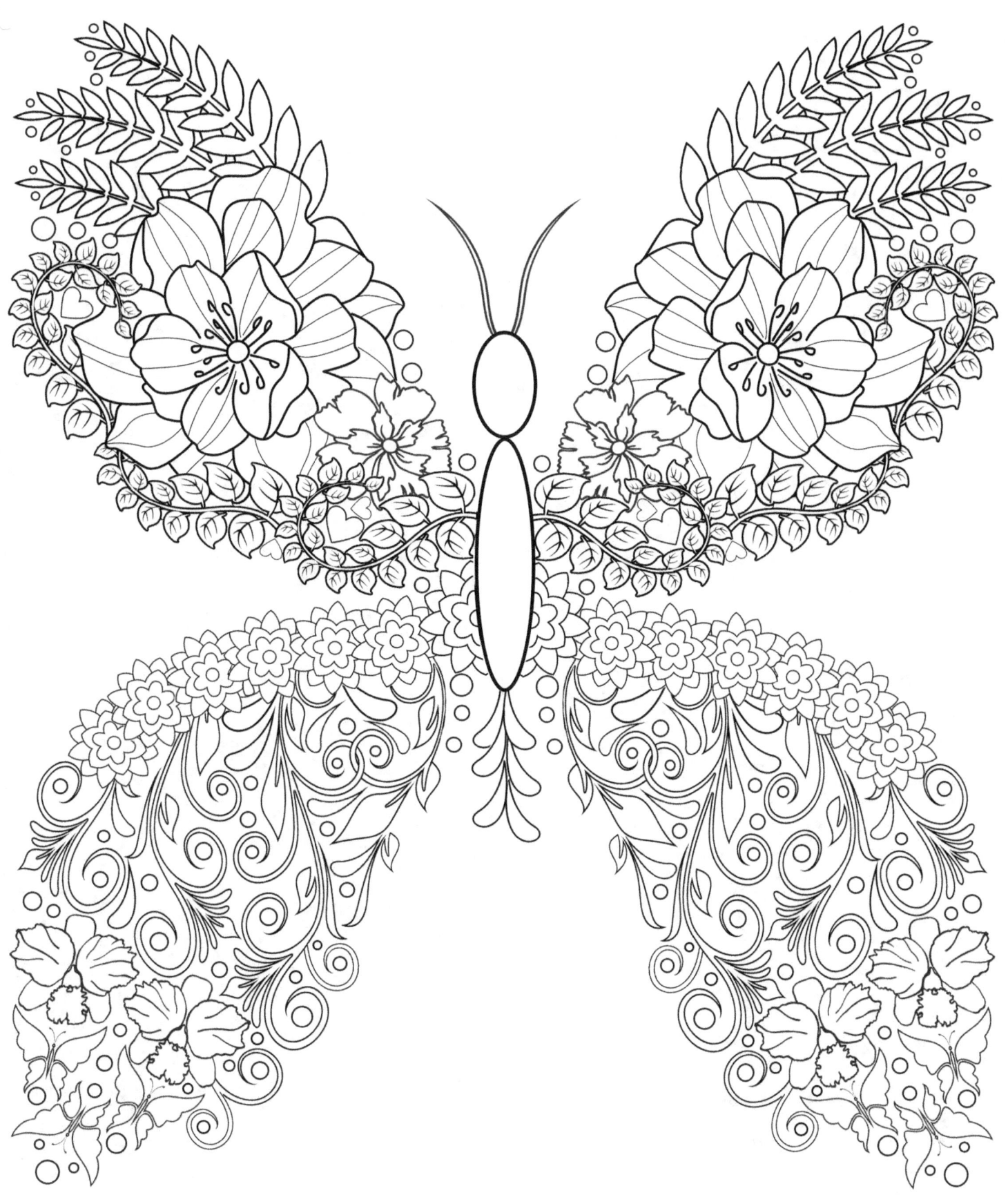

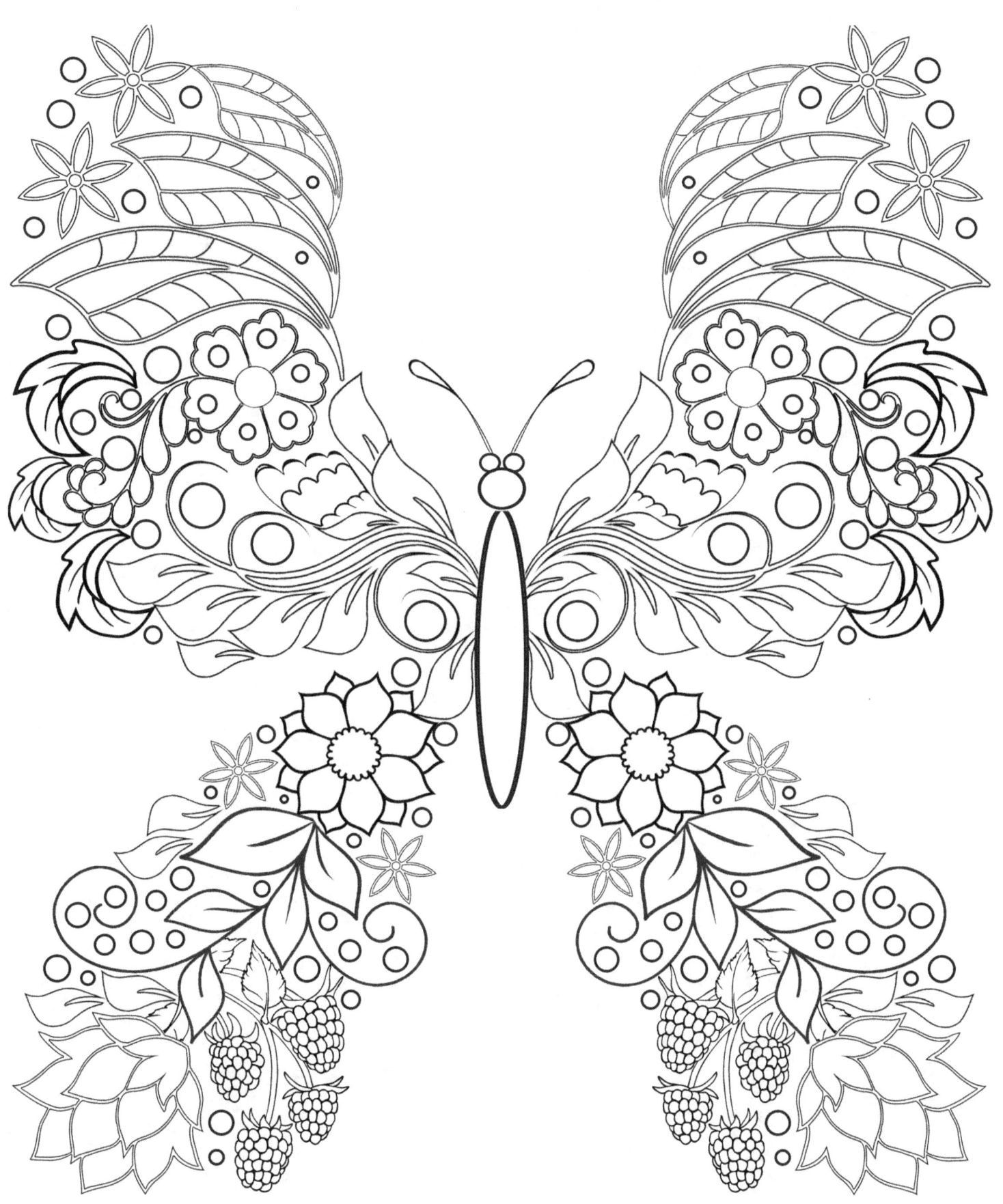

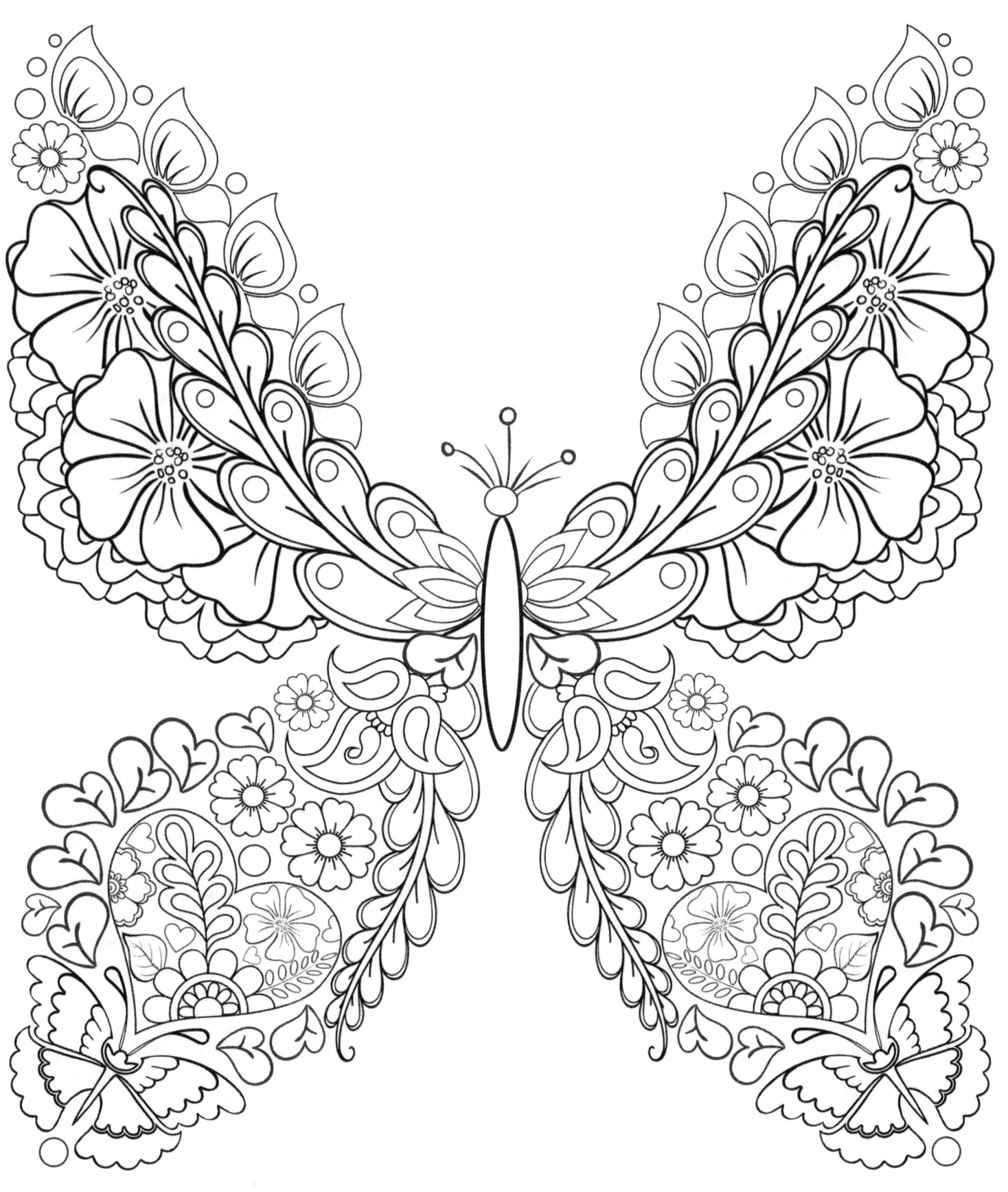

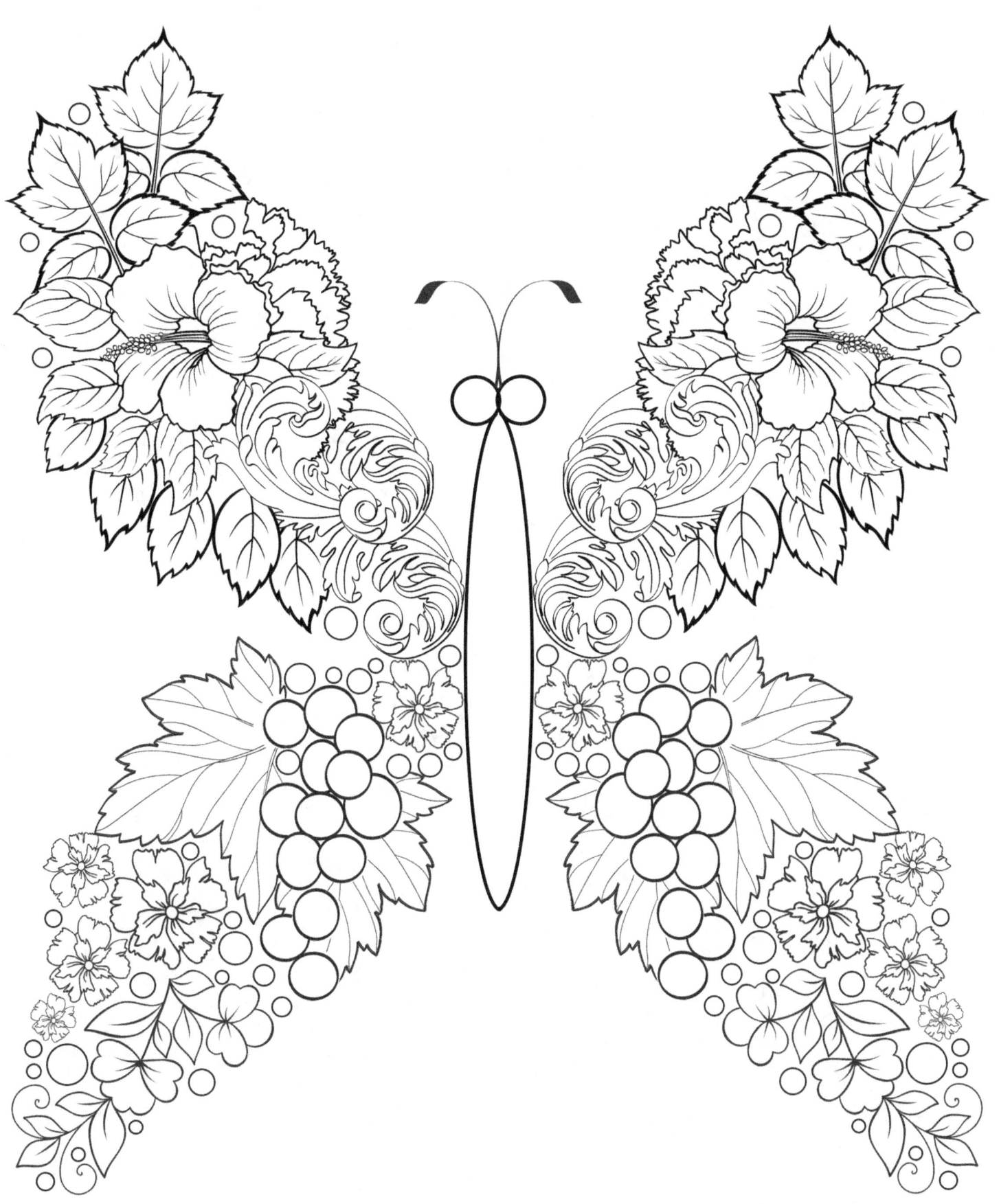

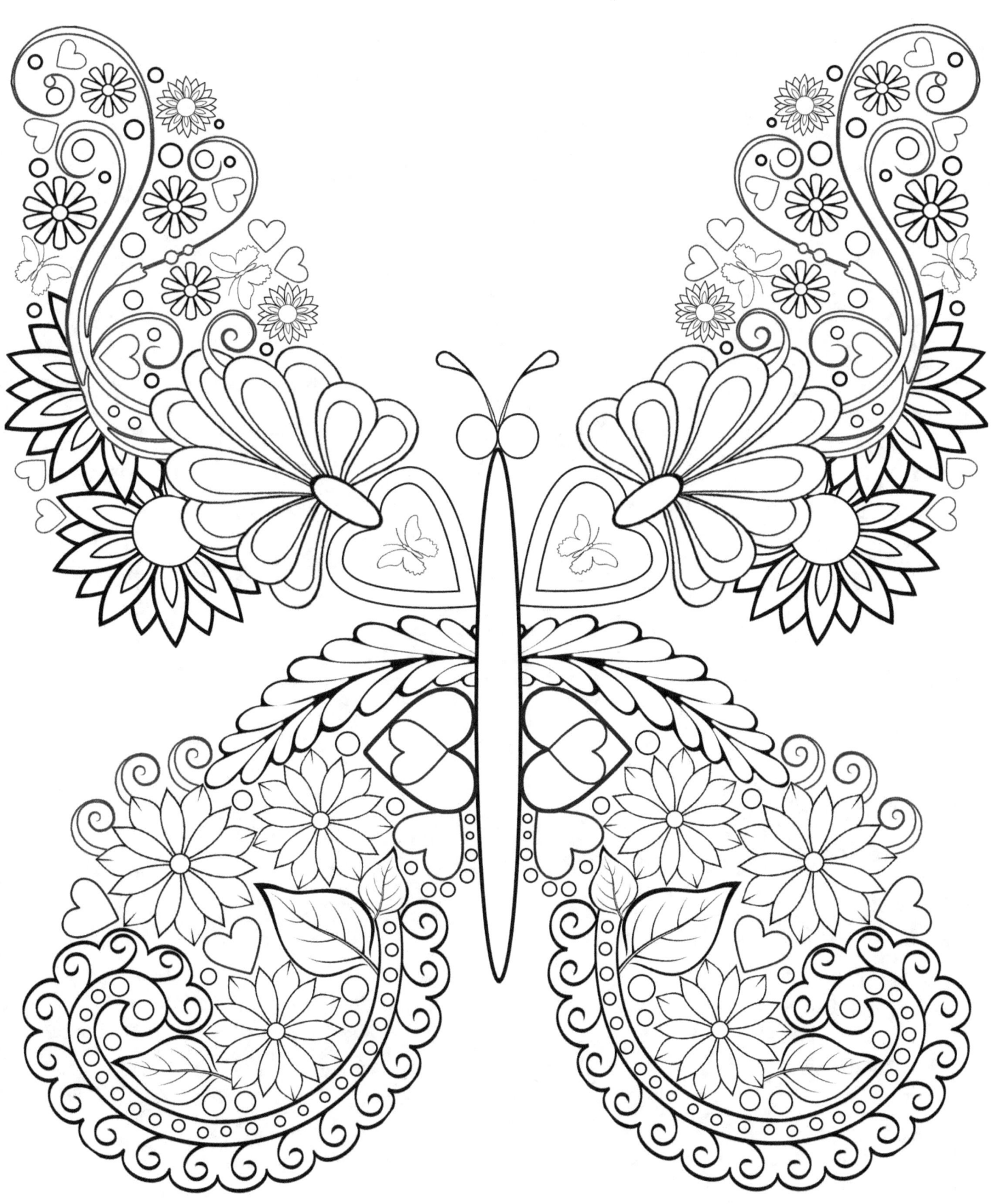

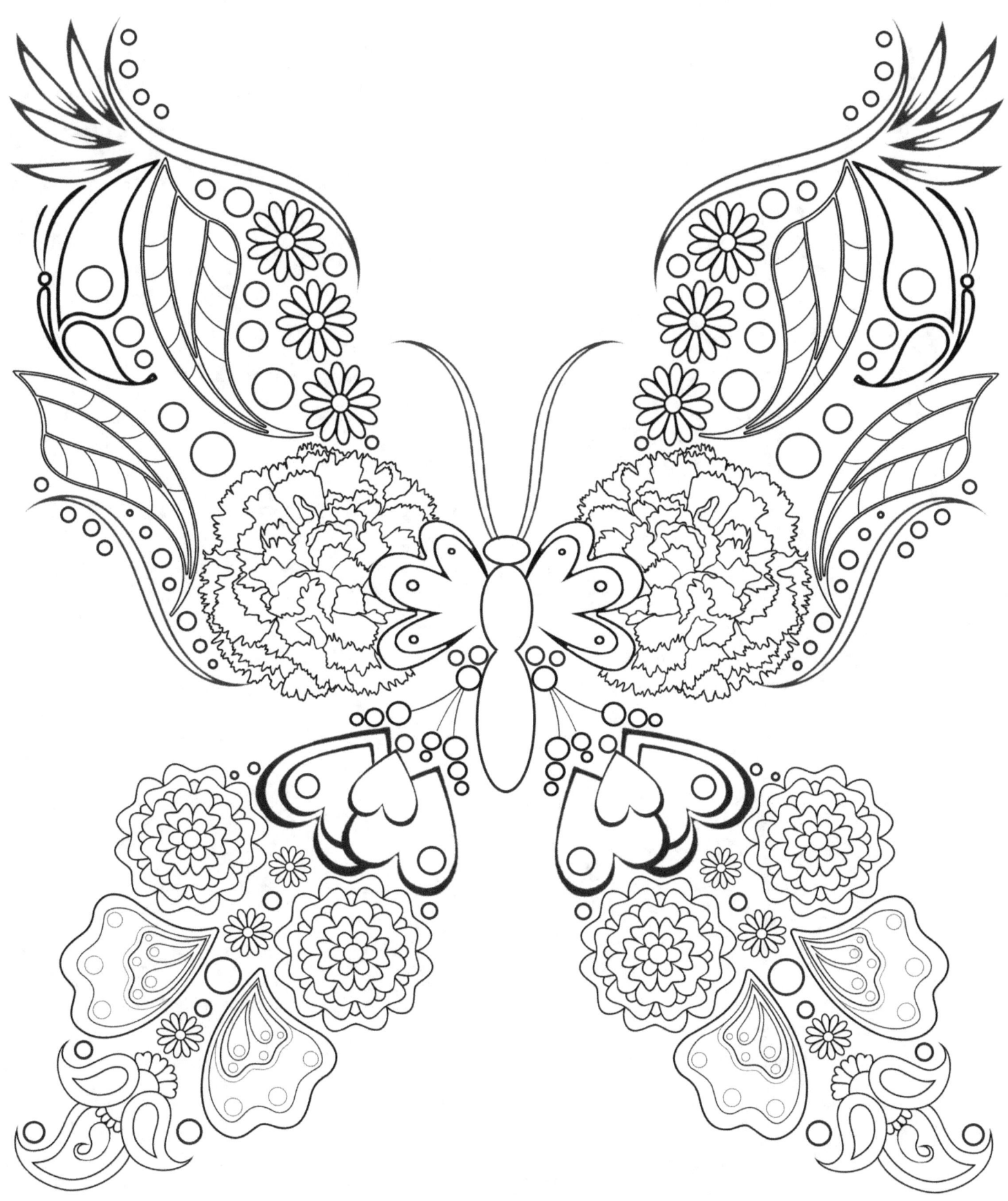

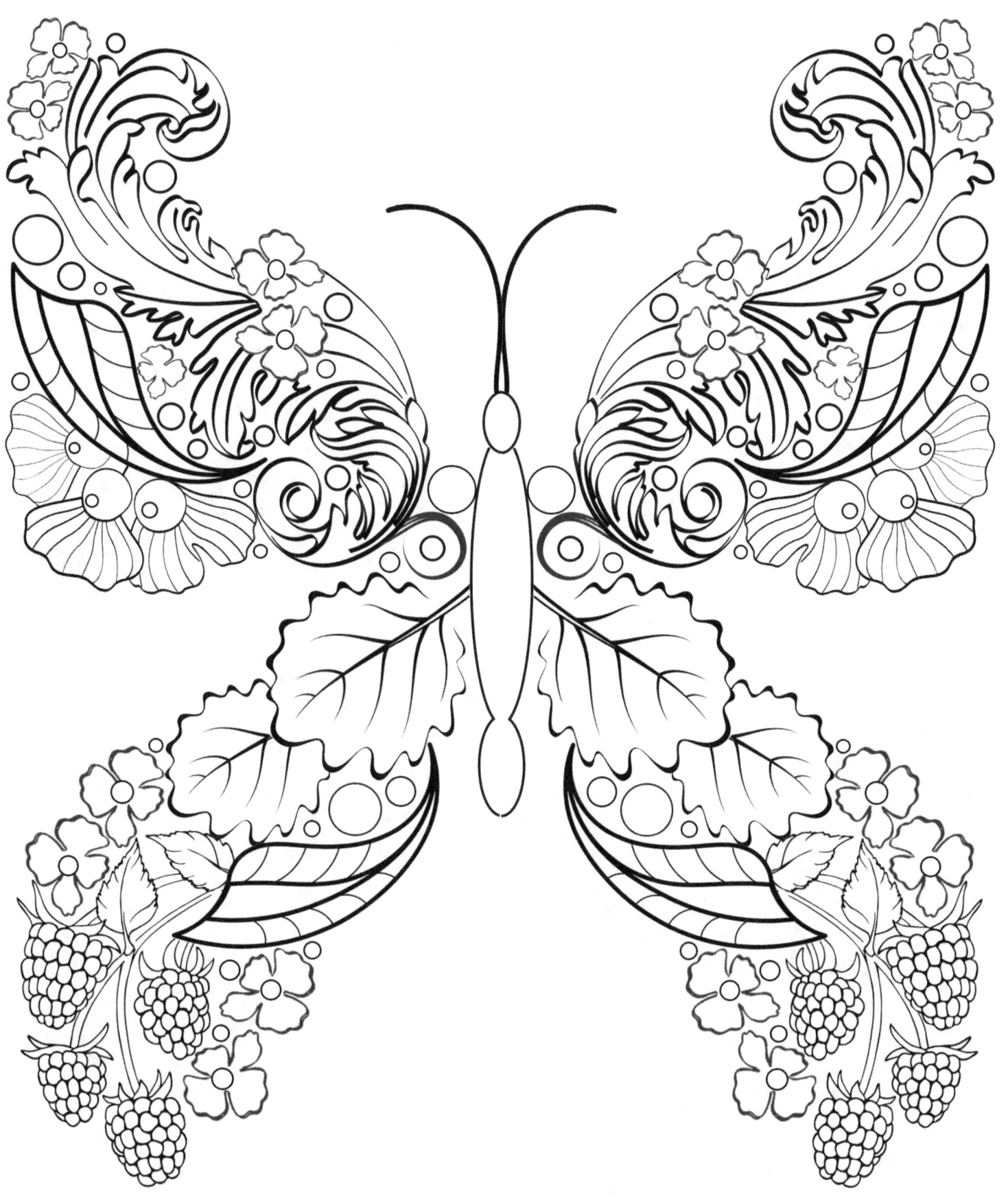

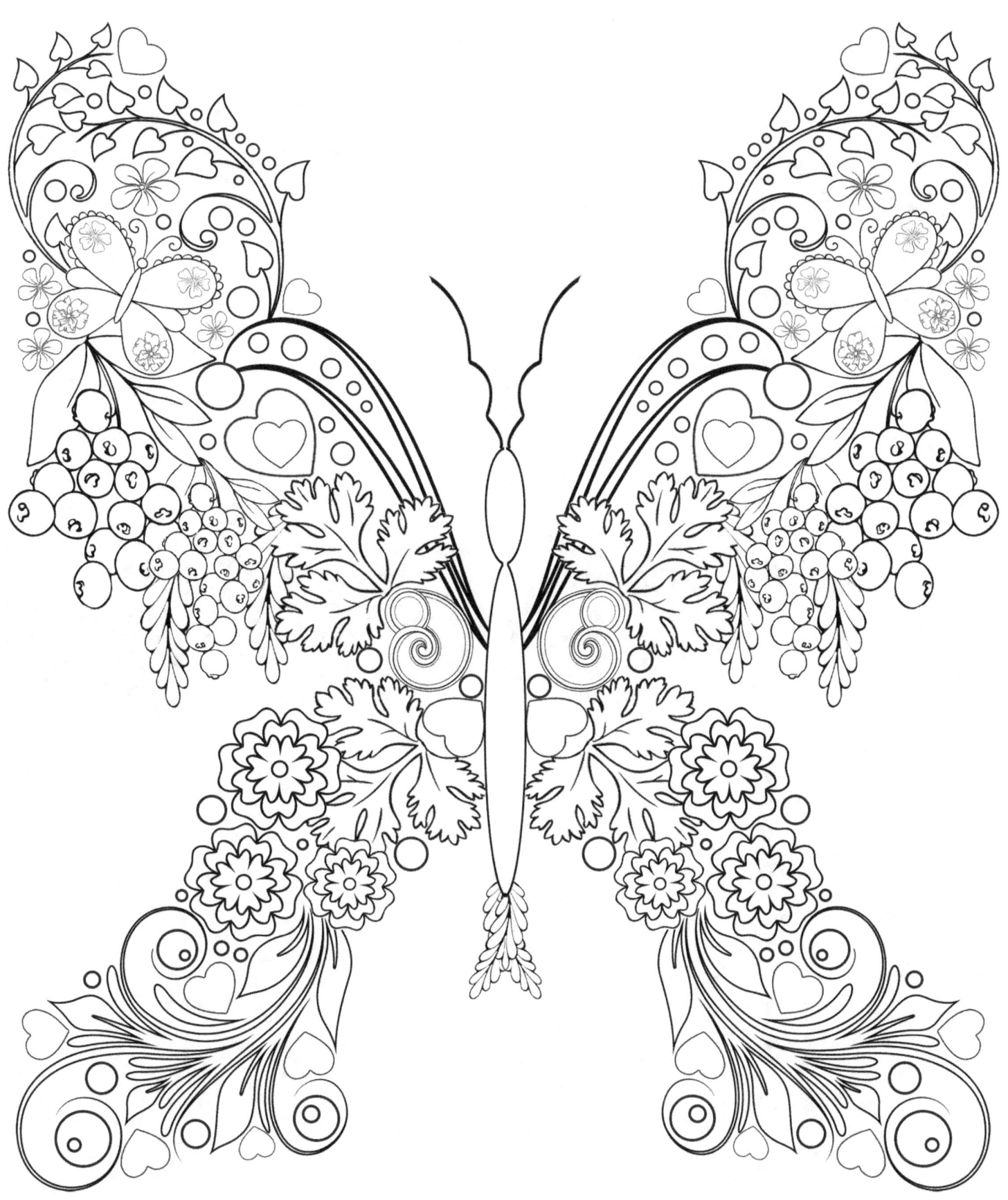

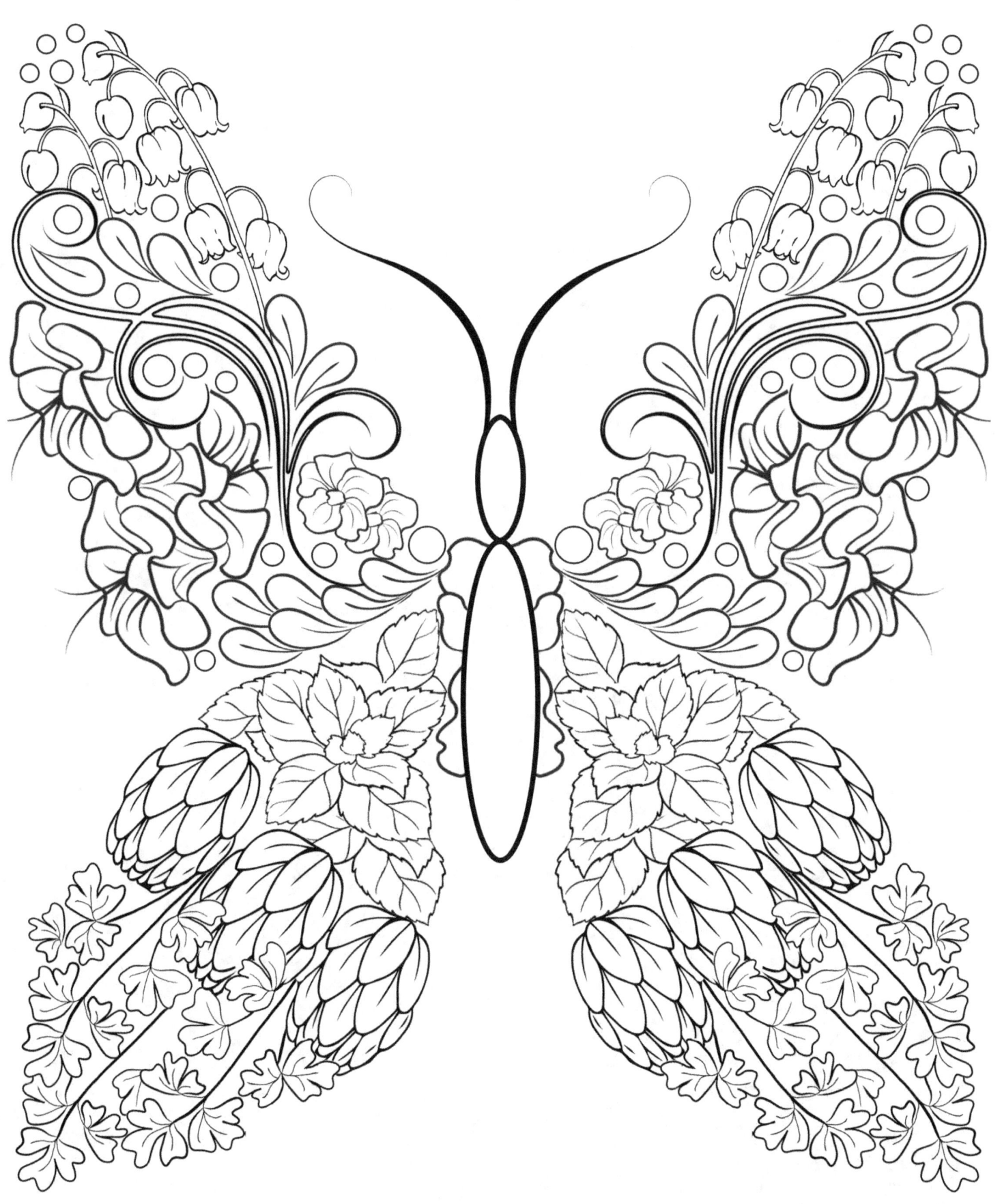

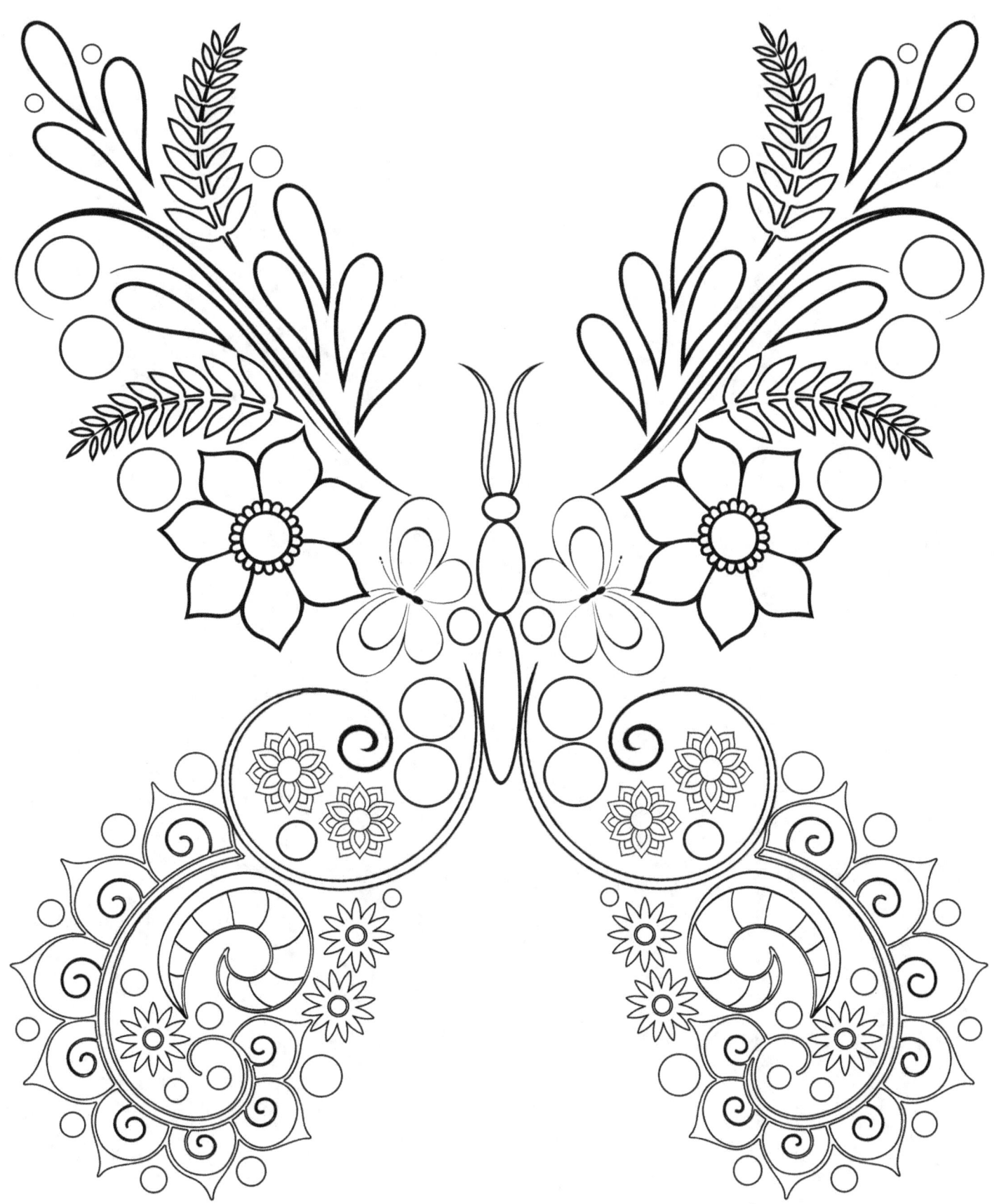

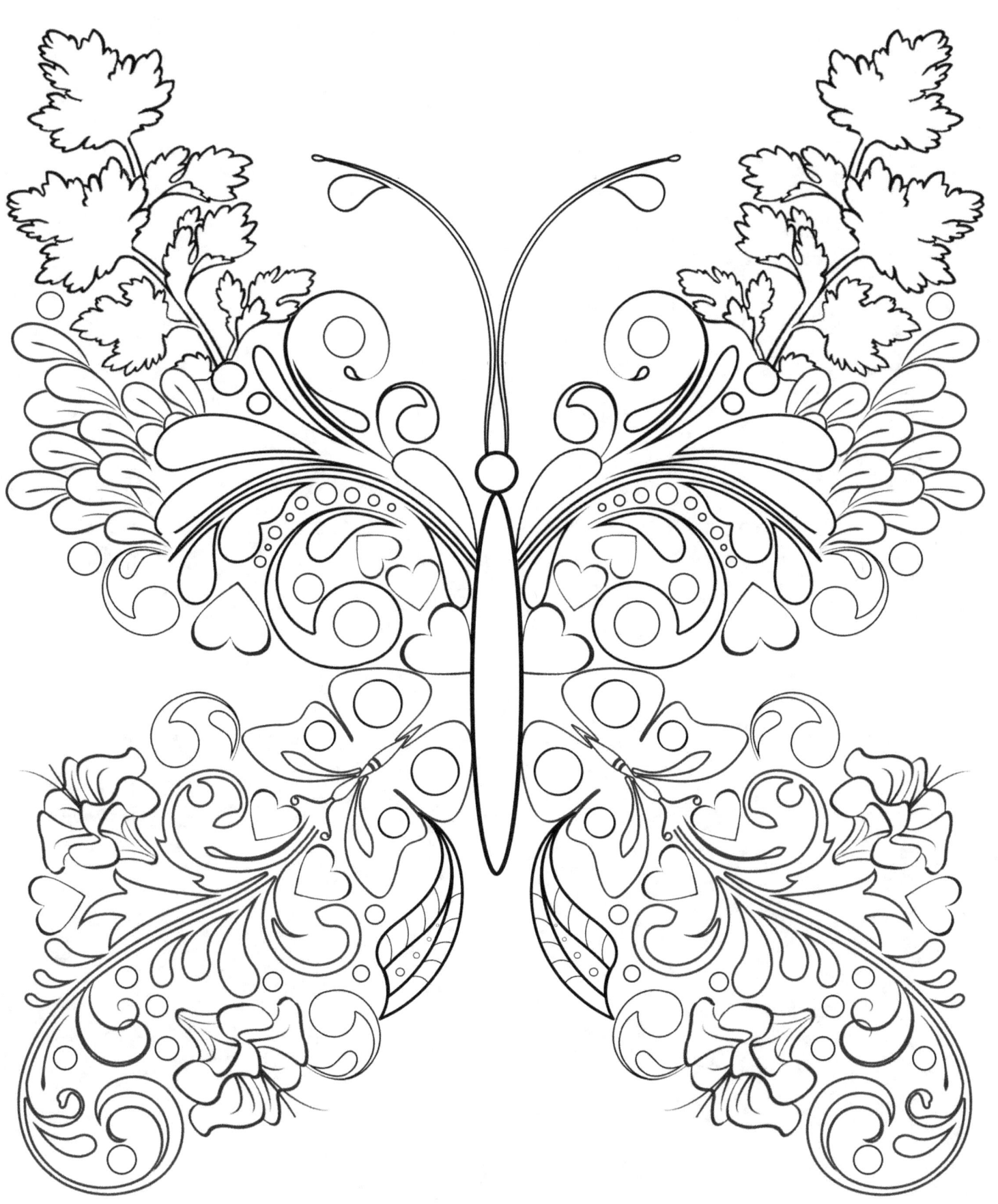

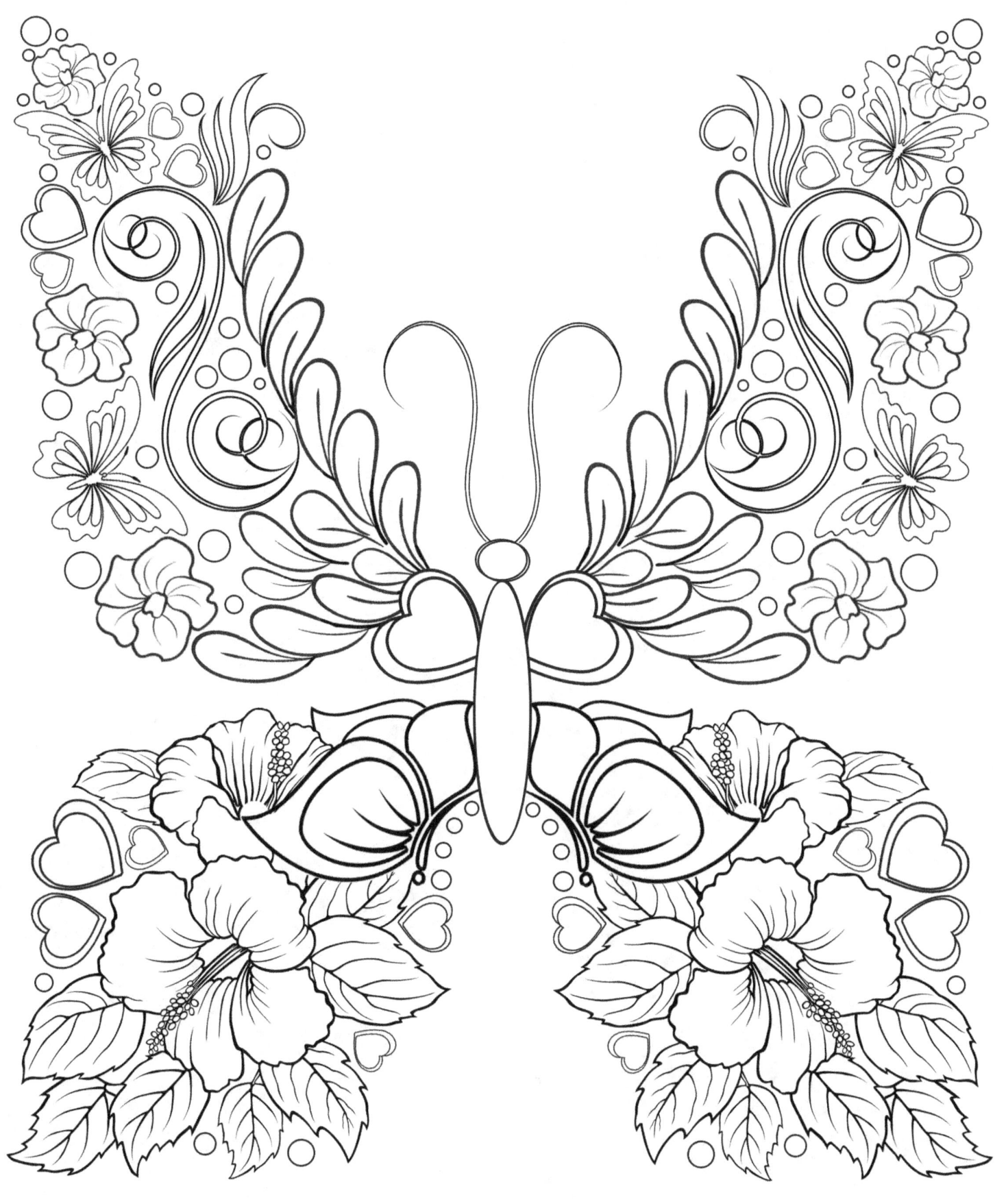

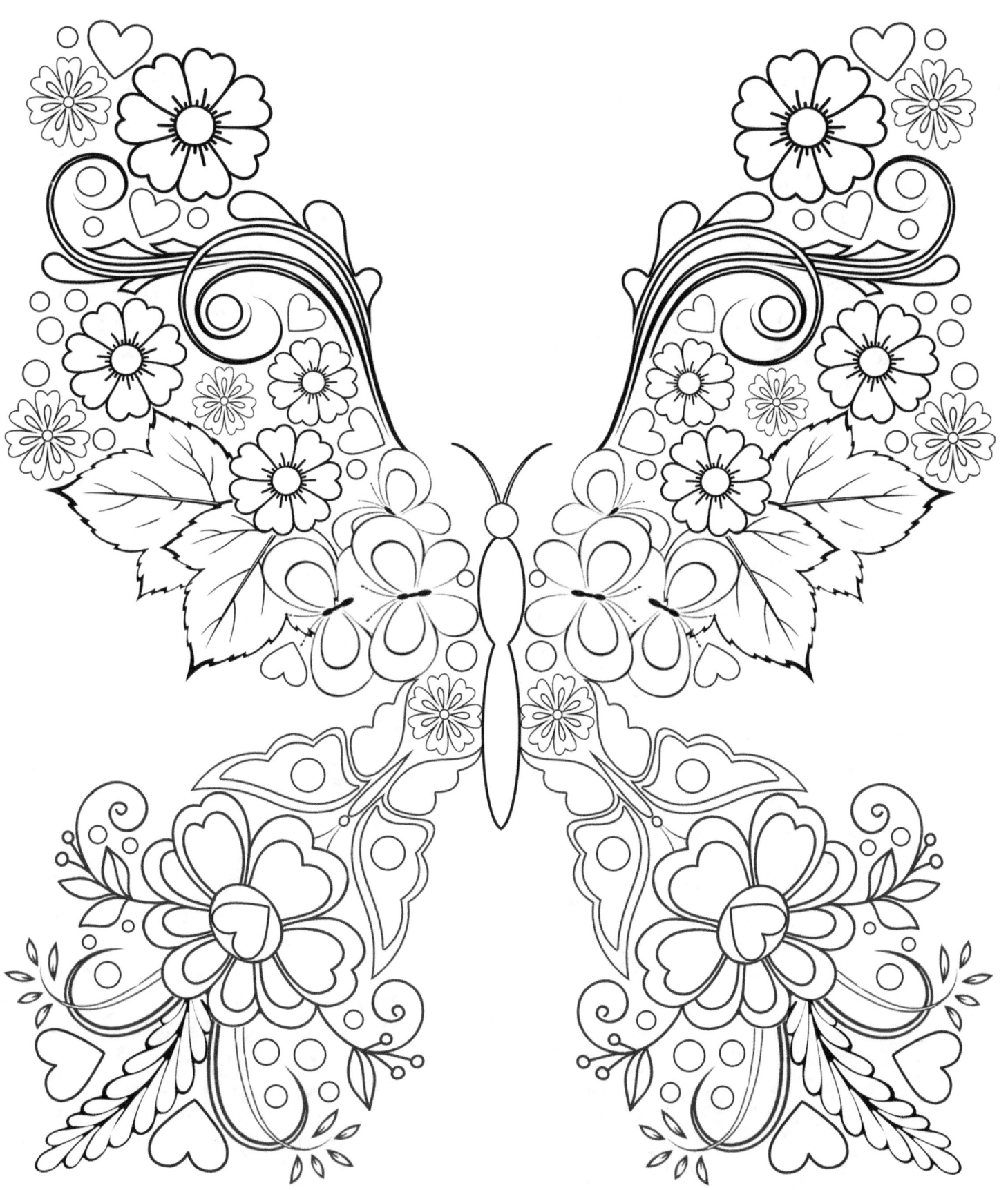

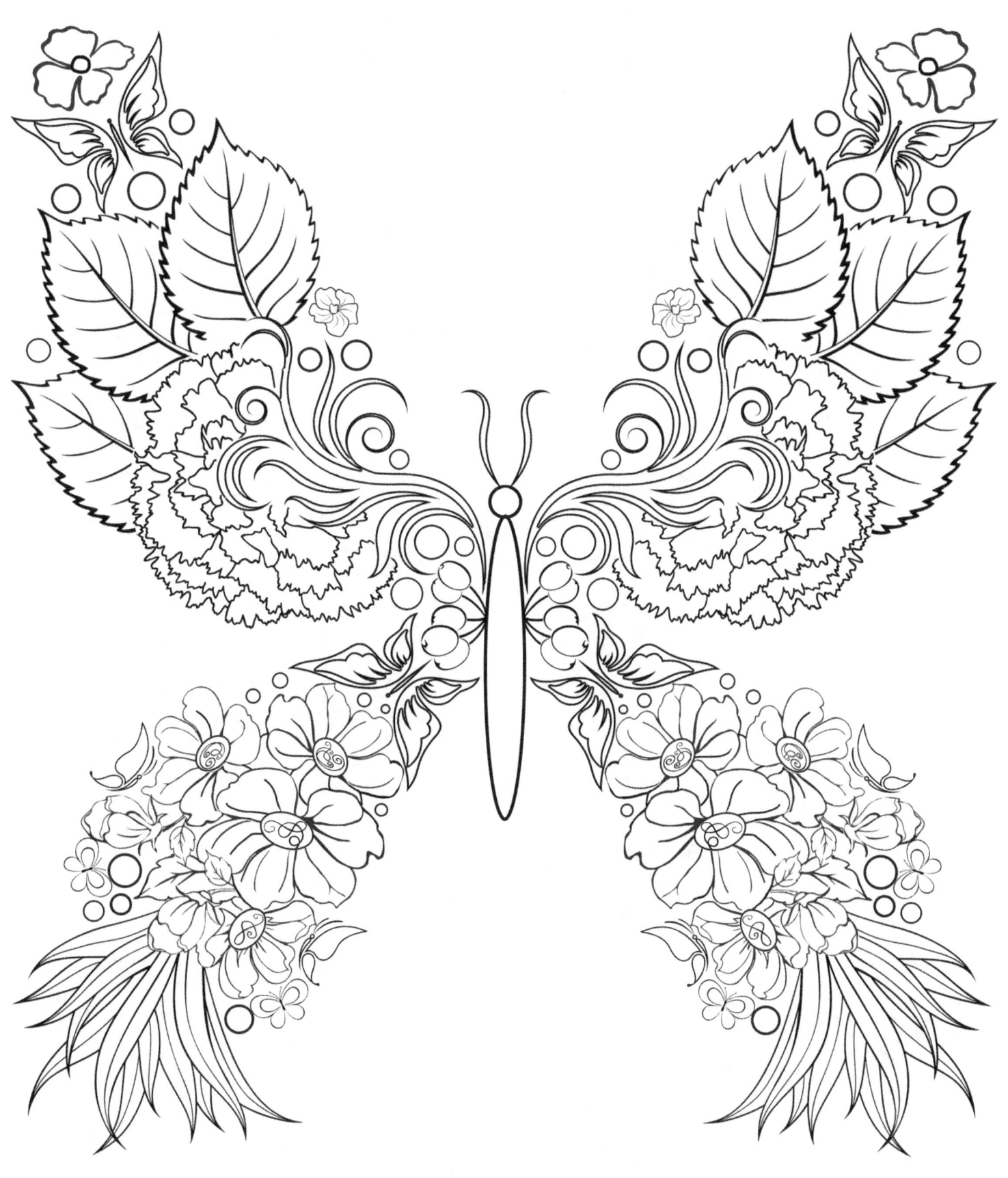

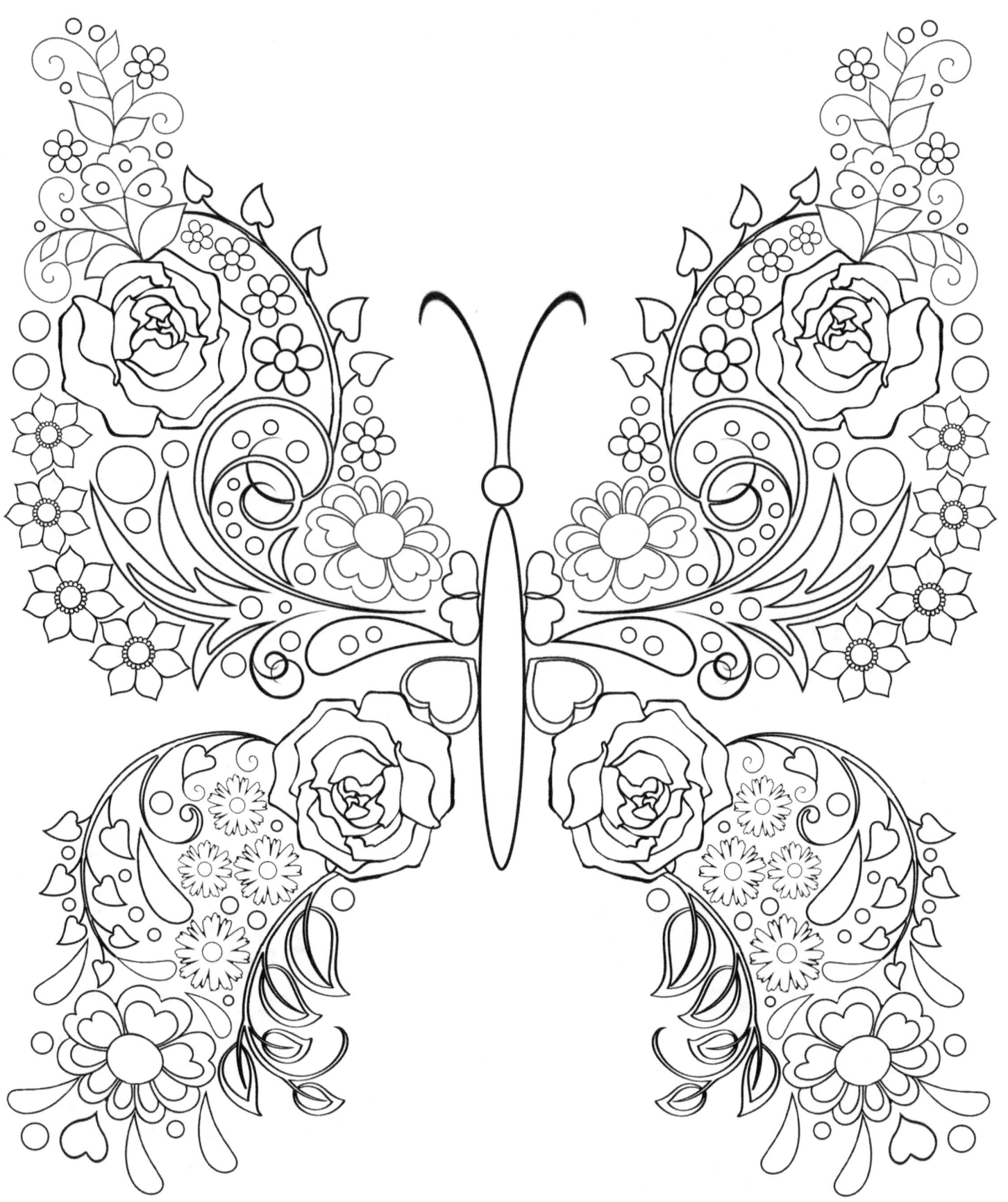

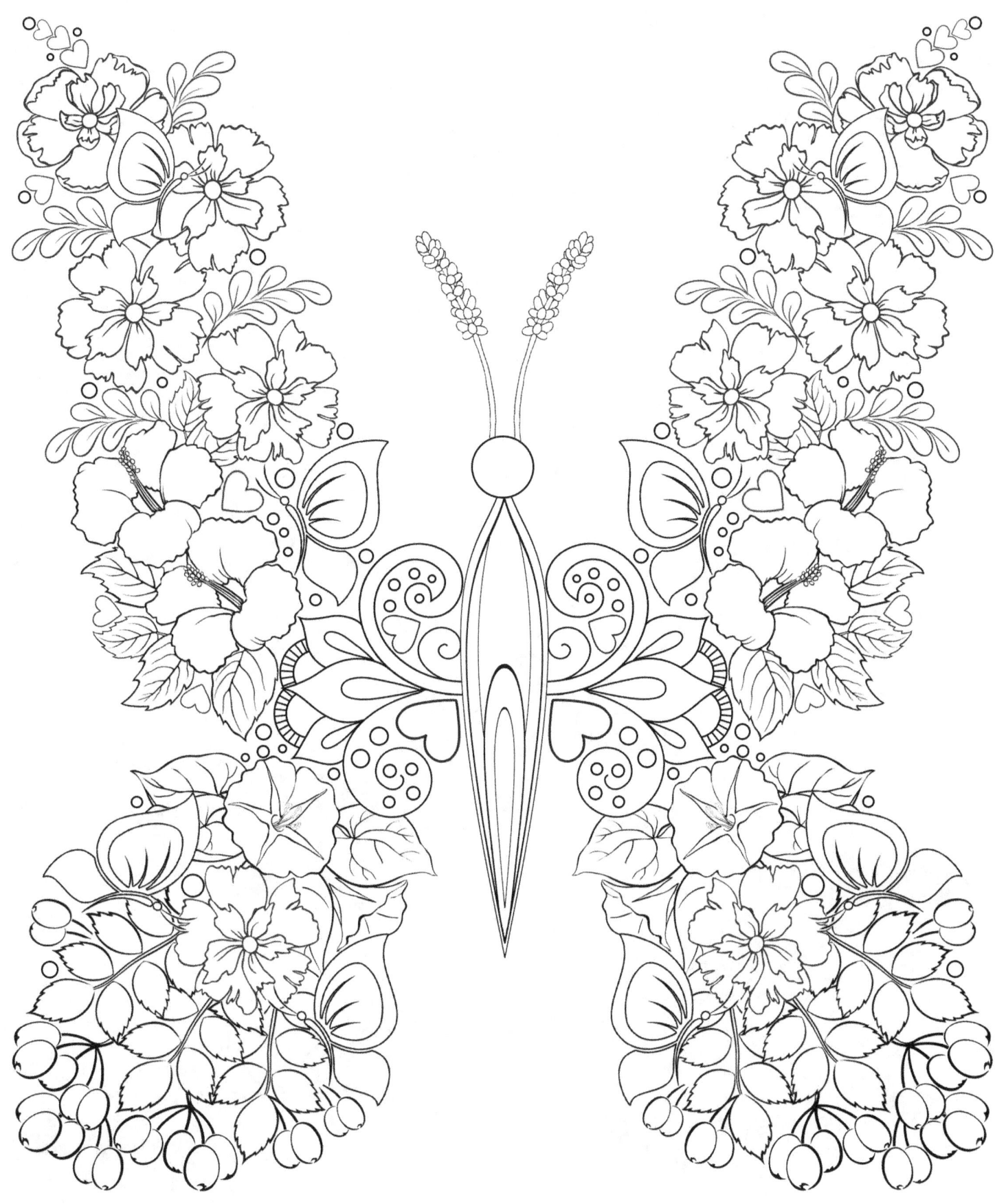

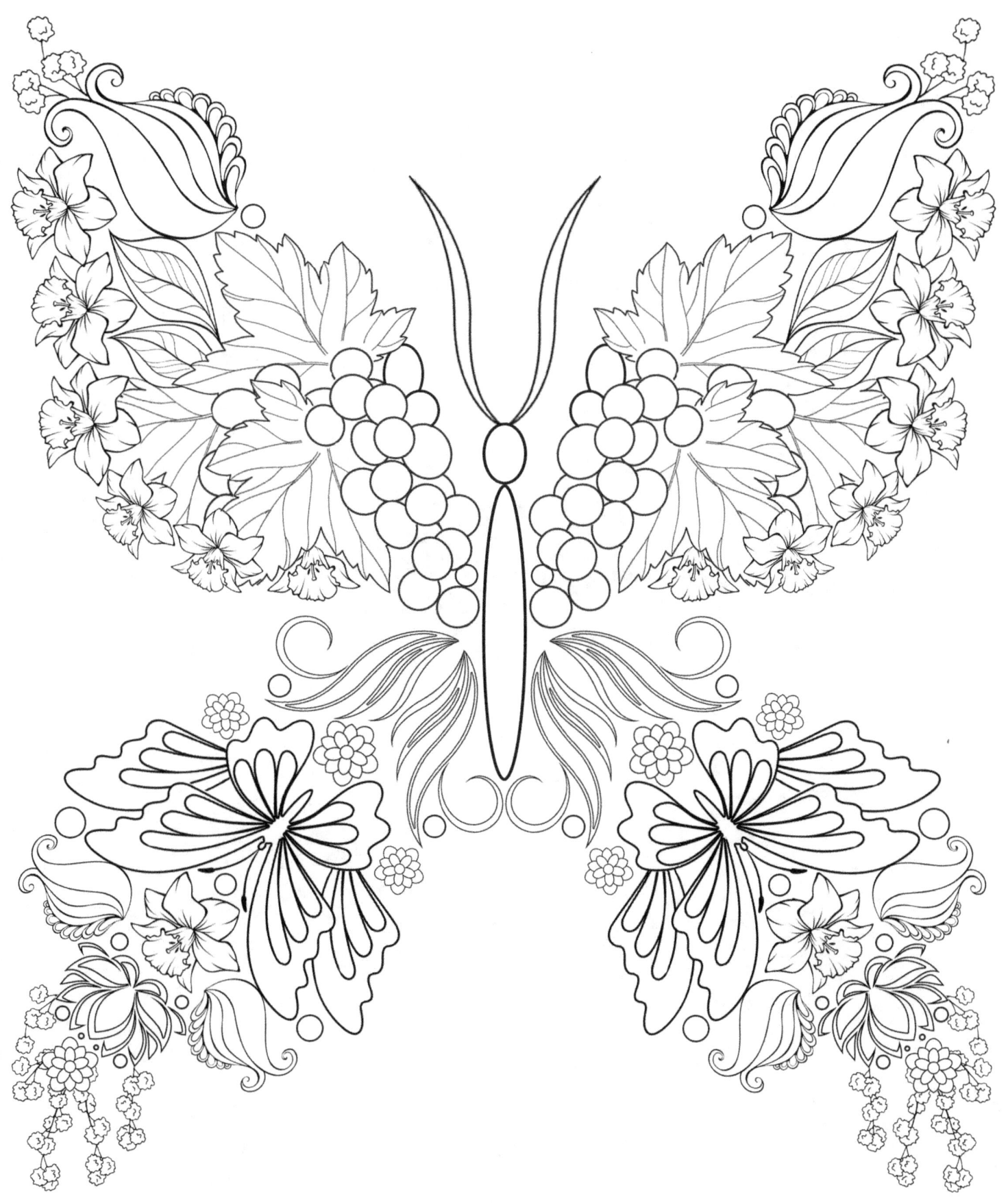

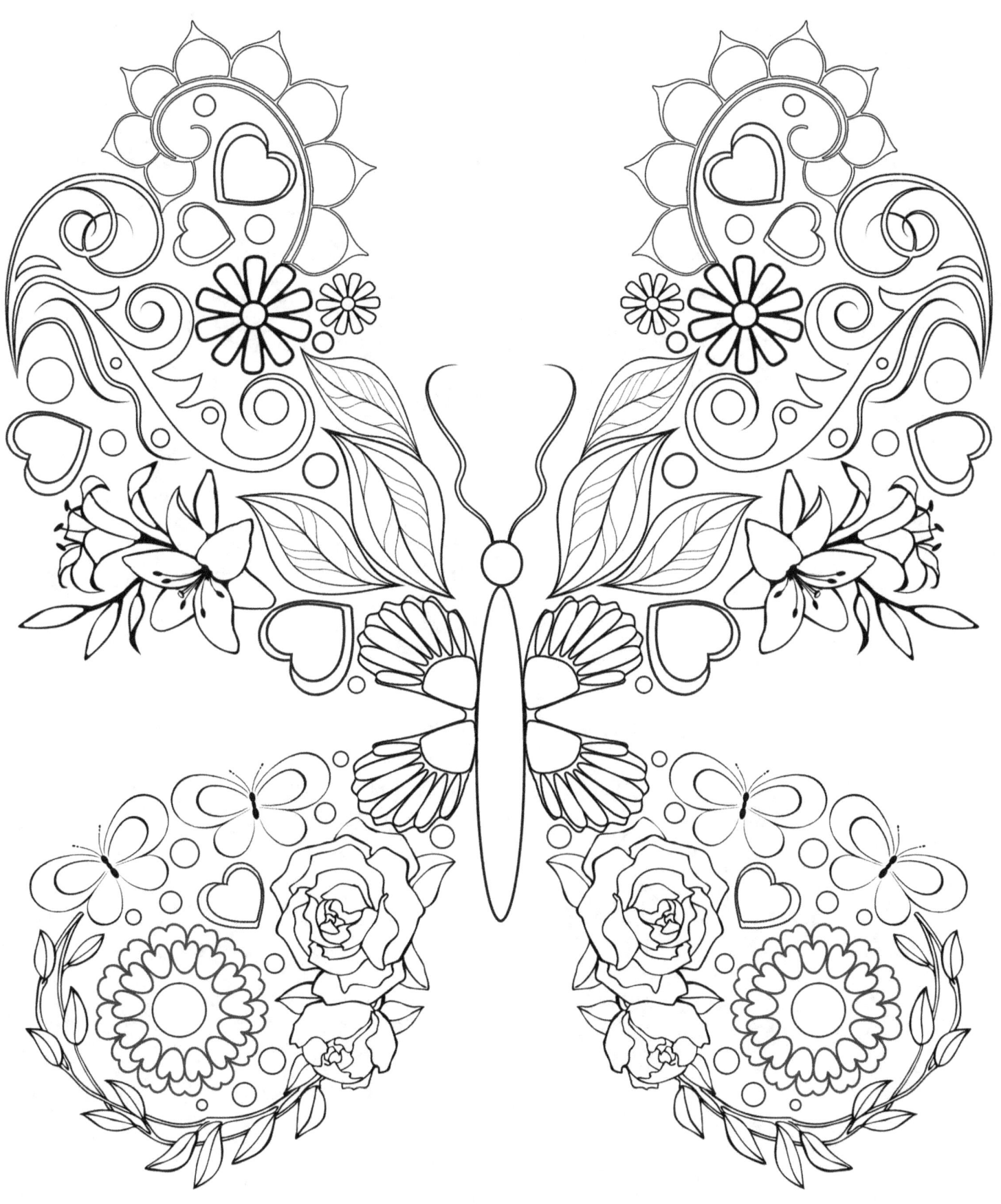

Other coloring books from Cozart Creative

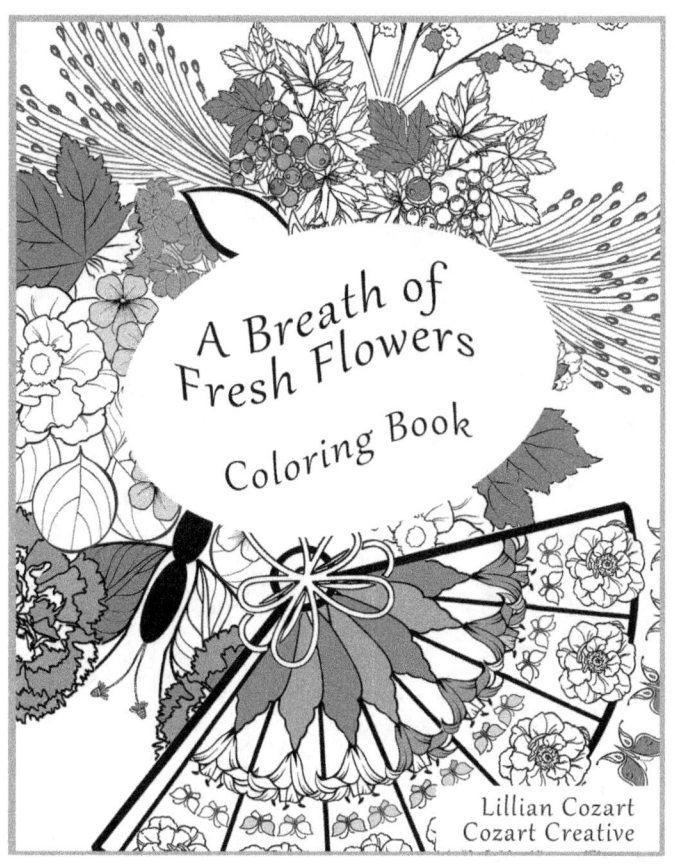

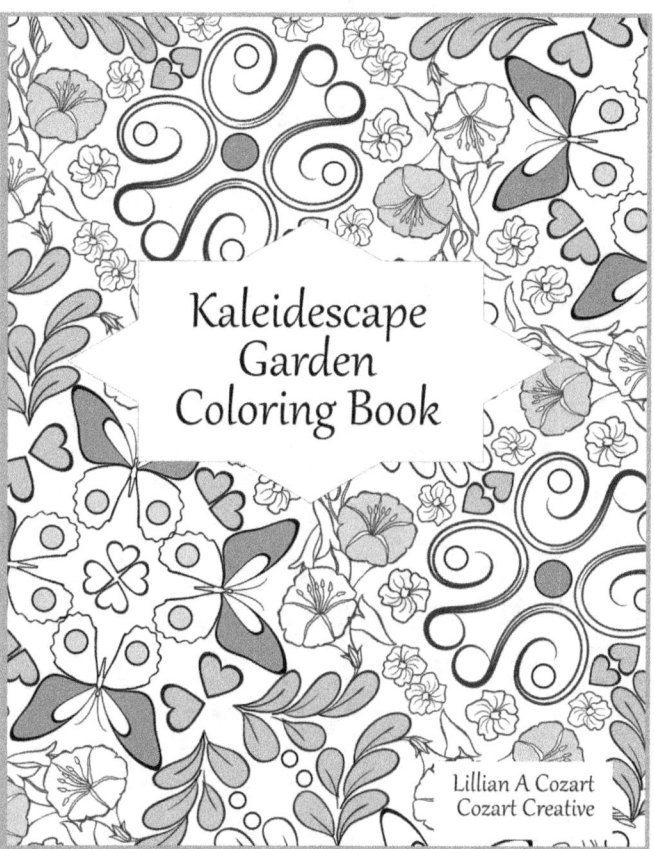

Visit www.cozartcreative.com to preview these coloring books, read articles, watch videos, learn techniques, get coloring supplies, and more!

Etsy: https://www.etsy.com/shop/CozartCreative
Twitter: twitter.com/CozartCreative
Facebook: www.facebook.com/CozartCreativeColoringBooks
Pinterest: www.pinterest.com/cozartcreative/

www.ingramcontent.com/pod-product-compliance
Lightning Source LLC
Chambersburg PA
CBHW081743220526
45468CB00008B/2215